INFORMATION ACCESS AND ADAPTIVE TECHNOLOGY

Carmela Cunningham
Norman Coombs

AMERICAN COUNCIL ON EDUCATION ★
ORYX PRESS ★
Series on Higher Education
1997

The rare Arabian oryx is believed to have inspired the myth of the unicorn. This desert antelope became virtually extinct in the early 1960s. At that time several groups of international conservationists arranged to have 9 animals sent to the Phoenix Zoo to be the nucleus of a captive breeding herd. Today the oryx population is over 1,000, and over 500 have been returned to the Middle East.

© 1997 by American Council on Education and The Oryx Press
Published by The Oryx Press
4041 North Central at Indian School Road
Phoenix, Arizona 85012-3397

This publication is also available in ASCII on a 3.5-inch diskette, formatted for Macintosh computers (ISBN 1-57356-124-X) or for IBM-compatible computers (ISBN 1-57356-125-8). Please contact The Oryx Press for more information.

Published simultaneously in Canada
Printed and bound in the United States of America

∞ The paper used in this publication meets the minimum requirements of the American National Standard for Information Sciences—Permanence of Paper for Printed Library Materials, ANSI Z39.48-1984.

Library of Congress Cataloging-in-Publication Data
Cunningham, Carmela
    Information access and adaptive technology / by Carmela Cunningham and Norman Coombs.
    p. cm. — (Series on higher education)
    Includes bibliographical references and index.
    ISBN 0-89774-992-8 (alk. paper)
    1. Computers and the handicapped—United States. 2. Handicapped college students—Services for—United States. 3. Self-help devices for the disabled—United States. 4. Communication devices for the disabled—United States. I. Coombs, Norman. II. American Council on Education. III. Title. IV. Series.
HV1569.5.C86 1997   97-11048
362.4'0483—DC21   CIP

This book is dedicated
to the inventors of the personal computer
and to the visionaries who developed
the adaptive hardware and software technology
that has transformed the personal computer
into a gateway to the Information Age
for people with disabilities.

CONTENTS

FOREWORD

Computers are providing a large proportion of our society increased power in the production, distribution, and manipulation of information. Computers are tools, and humans have always developed and used tools to improve work capacity whether by increasing strength, speed, or precision in performing tasks, or by decreasing the amount of energy needed to perform an activity. Tools, then, address our human limitations. Computers, like all other tools, have increased the capabilities of humans, allowing us to acquire information faster, manipulate it, and retransmit it to others without leaving our computer workstations.

People with disabilities may have benefited more from the proliferation of computers over the past two decades than any other population group. Computer technology provides these individuals the tools needed to obtain a significant increment of independence and productivity hitherto unavailable to them.

To experience and enjoy these benefits, people with disabilities must have access to, and be trained on, computers that are equipped with the essential adaptations that provide independent ability to perform data entry and to access the display of information. When these individuals have regular use of computers and appropriate adaptive technology, they can begin to benefit from the educational resources in our society that will permit them to become full participants in our economic enterprise.

At the threshold of the new millennium, we continually hear references to the fact that all citizens in our culture will be severely disadvantaged (if not handicapped) if they do not have an adequate education and mastery of computer technology. For people with disabilities, these two elements to independence and success are now closely intertwined. The publication of a volume addressed primarily to education professionals in an effort to assist them in meeting the technological and educational needs of students who have disabilities is both crucial and timely. The authors state that this book was written primarily for those working in higher education facilities—including faculty, computer services, librarians, disabled student services, and administrators. In a real way, these education professionals can be considered the gatekeepers to the future for many students with disabilities because education controls the boundaries of participation in our society. With a solid education (mediated by the essential adapted computer technology), multiple career options will be open to them, permitting them to flourish independently in the twenty-first century. In contrast, without a sound education or appropriate vocational training, many of these individuals with disabilities will languish unnecessarily in despair and dependence, often as charges of our welfare programs.

It is important, then, that people in educational and training facilities have the knowledge needed to assist their students with disabilities in obtaining and using the tools that will permit them to attain the highest level of independent performance possible.

With the guidance contained in this volume, education professionals can obtain the knowledge that will transform inaccessible electronic-based instructional materials, media, educational technology, and science laboratories into friendly and exciting learning environments for all students, including those with disabilities. It should be emphasized that improving the learning environment and style of teaching to meet the educational needs of students with disabilities typically has been found to improve the learning experience for all students.

Although specific information contained in this volume regarding existing technology will be time-sensitive, the recommendations on human behavior and understanding are not. Technology is rapidly evolving, but human values remain relatively constant over time. Knowledge is important, but action is critical. Translating the information gleaned by readers from this book into positive actions on campus and interactions with students with special needs should result in a much better educational experience and a higher quality of life in the future for many students.

Lawrence A. Scadden
Senior Program Director
Science Education for Students with Disabilities
National Science Foundation

PREFACE

The personal computer, when adapted with the necessary specialized hardware and software, enables individuals with disabilities to become fully effective participants in the new Information Age. They are transformed from individuals with disabilities into workers, students, and citizens with abilities. The purpose of this book is to describe the vast array of adaptive computer hardware and software that puts computer users with disabilities on a level playing field with everyone else.

I am a history professor, and I am blind. This technology has empowered and liberated me in both my personal life and in my professional activities. Not only has my work output increased significantly, but adaptive computing and telecommunications together have enabled me to be one of the pioneers in the popular field of distance learning. I have become connected with scores of skilled professionals with a variety of disabilities for whom adaptive computer technology has similarly enlarged their worlds and their opportunities. I hope that reading this book will enlist you as a friend and supporter in this unusual technological revolution.

By the time you complete this book, I want you to have a new awareness of how modern technology provides individuals with disabilities the tools to help themselves. In the Information Age, mental ability counts more than does physical disability. I also want you to know what adaptive computing is and how it works. You will have at your fingertips a list of resources that you can use to learn more about how to provide an adapted computer system to a school or work site, or how to adapt a computer for yourself or a friend.

The book was written primarily for educators in colleges and universities, including computer staff, librarians, disabled student services staff, teachers, and administrators. The book is also aimed at public school personnel so that their graduates will arrive at college ready to compete with their classmates who do not have disabilities. Additionally, it provides valuable information for employers, who need to be prepared to integrate workers with disabilities into their businesses. Individuals with disabilities will find a wealth of useful material in these pages, as will readers whose primary interest is in computers and how they function in society.

In the chapters that follow, we set forth an overview of adaptive computing. We are not providing technical details about either hardware or software. Technical terms will be explained, and jargon will be avoided whenever possible.

EASI (Equal Access to Software and Information) has been collecting and disseminating information about adaptive computing since the organization's creation in 1988. EASI began as a project within EDUCOM, a consortium of colleges and universities dedicated to integrating computing into higher education. EASI became an affiliate of the American Association for Higher Education in 1993. Carmela Cunningham and I have been actively involved in EASI activities for many years, and this work has provided us with valuable knowledge and useful experiences on which this book is based. EASI consists of friends and members from across the United States, as well as people from more than 40 other countries. We owe a debt to all of these people for what they have shared with us. The major part of the information included in this book is based on a seminar series that EASI created with the help of adaptive computing professionals from around the world. This project involved diligent work over a three-year period by a number of individuals (identified in the acknowledgments section).

The world of computer technology changes so rapidly that a new and revolutionary breakthrough is outmoded by the time it reaches the market, and information about this technology is similarly obsolete by the time it gets into print. New vendors and providers of hardware and software start up and disappear with a similar rapidity. Writing a comprehensive book that describes in detail the technology and how to use it is like trying to hit a moving target—and that is not what we attempt here. We will, however, provide a broad introduction to the issues involved in providing adaptive computing services, with examples of how it is changing lives and how it is being provided in various institutional and commercial settings. We will also introduce you to an extensive list of resources where you can obtain information that is constantly updated.

Our goals in this book are (1) to introduce you to the social, economic, and legal reasons that your institution should provide adaptive services; (2) to give you guidance in how to set up, staff, and maintain an adaptive computing lab or workstation; (3) to give you guidance in linking people with the adaptive technology that will be helpful to them; (4) to introduce you to the potential of the Internet and other electronic information resources; and (5) to discuss other specific areas in which individuals will benefit from the use of adaptive computing technology, such as in the library and in the fields of science, engineering, and math. We will also talk about social issues that arise as people with disabilities participate fully in our society.

Like the changes in technology, the legal issues discussed in this book are subject to change as the courts make new decisions on specific cases and as state and federal legislatures write new laws. We are not lawyers, and what we offer on this topic is meant only as an introduction. It should not be taken as legal counsel or advice. Our strongest recommendation is for organizations providing adaptive computing facilities to be proactive; to do more than they think the law requires, and to do it sooner than they believe is necessary. We hope you will do this not so much to avoid litigation as to provide opportunities for your students and employees.

Our goal as we present this material is to take a book about technology and humanize it. We have included short stories about people who have benefited in real, human ways from this technology. We also include descriptions of several different model adaptive computing configurations to show how computer and information systems can be made accessible for persons with disabilities. Your situation will be unique, so we cannot provide a set of rules or a design that will automatically work for you. However, we believe that by exposing you to how different schools and organizations have addressed their problems with unique solutions, we can help you design a system that will meet the needs of your campus, students, workplace, and employees. The resource lists and examples included in many chapters are supplemented by the material in the appendixes, which will point you toward even more information and help that will make your efforts to provide services most beneficial.

Norman Coombs

ACKNOWLEDGMENTS

This book is based on the work of EASI (Equal Access to Software and Information), which provided the experience and knowledge that have enabled the authors to produce it. EASI's outreach has relied on the support of both the American Association for Higher Education and EDUCOM. These organizations provided invaluable assistance to EASI in its work of disseminating information about adaptive computing to schools and universities. We owe a special thanks to Steve Gilbert, Ruth Holder, and Ellen Shortill for their loyalty and encouragement.

The authors wish to express their deep gratitude to the many people from around the world who contributed to the activities of EASI, both in person and over the Internet. The examples of courage and triumph over adversity and the technical information that they have shared are woven through the pages of this volume.

The book is based on materials produced for the EASI Adaptive Computer Seminar Series, and those people who worked on it deserve special notice. Daniel H. Chalfen, James Breene, Ellen Cutler, Jane Berliss, Carl Brown, Darren Gabbert, Allyn Rankin-Martines, Sheryl Burgstahler, Nils Peterson, James Knox, Barbara Heinisch, Ray Lovell, Gail Pickering, Harry Murphy, Dick Banks, Tom McNulty, Gayle Gagliano, Terri Muraski, Scott Lissner, Jeff Senge, David Lunney, John Gardner, Richard Jones, T. V. Raman, and Gregg Vanderheiden deserve a special thanks. Without their efforts, this book would not have had its present scope.

The authors want to express their personal thanks to Jean Coombs, Grant Young, and George Cunningham, all of whom helped in various ways— reading, editing, advising, and most of all providing understanding, love, and support through the entire process.

Carmela Cunningham
Norman Coombs

INTRODUCTION

I don't have a disability. Not on this day; not at this moment. What happens tomorrow, I can't guess. Chances are good that I, like most of the people in this country, won't become disabled in the next day. But some will. And, of course, there are 48 million people in the United States who already have one type of disability or another. I know some of them, and you probably know some of them too.

So, if I don't have a disability, why am I writing this book? The simple answer is that what this book talks about is vitally important. And what this book is going to help you do is right; it's morally, economically, and legally right. First, I'm going to tell you why, and then Norman Coombs and I are going to explain how to do these things that are so right.

As I noted above, there are 48 million disabled people in the United States. Their disabilities range from limited mobility because of things like heart attacks, sports injuries, and missing limbs, to people who can't quite hear what you're saying because they heard too much gunfire in Vietnam. There are people who have been blind since birth, and people who lost some or all of their sight later in life. People with speech problems, people with dyslexia, and people whose feet just won't do what their brains tell them to do. They've all got disabilities, and we all are subject to acquiring any one of those disabilities on any given day.

Forty-eight million people is getting awfully close to 20 percent of the total American population. That's almost one in every five people, and no matter how you slice it, that's a lot of people to tell they can't have their piece of the American pie. That's a lot of people to tell they can't have the education promised to every young person in this country, and that's a lot of people to tell they can't have a job to support themselves and their families. And besides the fact that it's not right to exclude people with disabilities, I know that I don't ever want to hear that I can't have a job, that I can't go into restaurants, and that I can't play the game the rest of the people play because someone slammed into me on the freeway and I can't walk anymore.

And that's all it would take to make me—or you—stop being able-bodied and start being disabled. I really hope it doesn't happen, but if it does, I hope that our society is big enough to still have a place for me and you. In the meantime, I'd like to make sure that we do what's right and make room for those other 48 million people.

Let's talk, too, about something that all educators and business operators care about—money. Why is providing access and reasonable accommodations for disabled employees a sound economic decision?

We decided a long time ago that as a society, we weren't going to let people who had a hard time taking care of themselves go without. So we have a host of public and private assistance programs that support people with disabilities. The taxes we all pay fund those programs. And because educational institutions—colleges and universities included—depend on tax dollars as well, these institutions have a vested interest in spending those tax dollars as efficiently as possible.

In 1990, the United States spent more than $120 billion through a variety of federal, state, and private support payment structures to assist people with disabilities. Those payments came in the form of Social Security Disability Income, Food Stamps, Medicaid, Medicare, Workmen's Compensation, insurance company payments, and direct payments from businesses. We spent another $3 billion that year in rehabilitation programs.

We spend billions of dollars to support people with disabilities. But the fact is that while we pay many of those people to sit at home, a large number of them can earn their own livelihoods. One-half of the disabled people in the United States are between the ages of 16 and 64—working age. Seventy-one percent of people with disabilities are unemployed. That's too many people for wage earners and businesses to support. That's too many people to deny the right to earn their own living.

If you still aren't convinced of the benefits of educating and hiring people with disabilities, then how about this? It's the law. If you don't provide "reasonable accommodations" for people with disabilities, you're in violation of the law—the Americans with Disabilities Act of 1990, to be specific.

What does the Americans with Disabilities Act of 1990 (ADA) require of colleges and universities as educational institutions and as employers? Educational institutions are required to provide individuals with disabilities equal access to all educational programs, equipment, and buildings. Reasonable accommodations must be made for every disabled student attending a college or university, and no student may be denied entrance to a college or university based on a disability.

Colleges and universities must also comply with the same ADA mandates as any other employer. First, the ADA forbids an employer to deny employment to a disabled person who is qualified to do a particular job. Second, it requires employers to make reasonable accommodations for disabled employees. Third, it imposes stiff penalties on employers who refuse to comply with the Act. Chapter 2 discusses the Americans with Disabilities Act in greater detail, but you should understand going into this that the ADA absolutely requires that you (1) hire qualified disabled people; and (2) make accommodations to allow disabled people to work for you. You will be fined if you fail to do those two things.

Now that I've told you why providing access is good for your school or business—and for society—Norman Coombs and I are going to concentrate on telling you how to provide accommodations, and more importantly, how to provide accommodations in the best possible way to get the most for every dollar you spend. I want you to make room on your campus for students and employees with disabilities, and I want the disabled people you educate and hire to be efficient and productive.

Your campus may have to put out extra effort and some extra dollars up front for people with disabilities, but if you do it right, your campus—and our society—will be able to reap the benefits of having provided a good education and an equitable workplace.

Now let's talk about doing it right.

Carmela Cunningham

CHAPTER 1

Higher Education's Obligations to People with Disabilities

Grant was born with·very low vision, but as a child and young man, he did most of the things that his friends did. He delivered newspapers, played the saxophone, took karate lessons, and spent as much time on the ski slopes as he could. At the age of 19, while making a last ski run for the day, he took a nasty fall—and broke his neck. Grant spent several months in the hospital and several more in a rehabilitation center. Then he was on his own. He moved into handicapped housing and spent his days collecting Social Security and hanging out with his buddies. A few years went by like that. Then one day, Grant signed up for a physical rehabilitation class at the local community college. He took it four times before he got up the nerve to register for regular academic courses. Using adapted computers and special software for his classwork, Grant earned a 4.0 grade point average and received his associate in arts degree. Then he transferred to a four-year university and got a part-time job working in the academic computing lab. The part-time job has turned into a full-time job.

For the first time ever, people with disabilities are demanding the same opportunities and services that are available to everyone else in America. This is especially true in schools and the workplace.

This cultural revolution is taking place at precisely the same time that America is reaching the peak of the Information Age, a period in which computer technology and electronic information are becoming·integral to our society. This technology has been a boon for people with disabilities. Adaptive input and output devices make it possible for people with any type of disability or combination of disabilities to manipulate and use computers, while special computing software and hardware packages have provided unprecedented ways for people with disabilities to accomplish tasks and access information. Computer technology has provided people with disabilities access to information, resources, equipment, and jobs that were closed to them not too many years ago.

DISABILITY AND ADAPTATION

Most of us do one or more things a little differently than other people. Some of us wear eyeglasses or contact lenses to see better. Some of us put cushions on our office chairs or on the seats of our cars so we can maneuver better or sit more comfortably. Some of us type everything because we don't like writing longhand.

If a person is in a situation where performing one or more functions in the *usual* way is a little difficult, no one thinks much about it if that person amends the situation or standard procedures a little to enhance performance. Most of us do it so often that we don't even consciously recognize that we're adapting a situation to fit our own needs—or disabilities. It's not really very clear where the line is that determines whether or not a person has a "disability"—but there is a legal definition.

The Americans with Disabilities Act of 1990 defines disability as "a physical or mental impairment that substantially limits one or more of the major life activities of such individual, a record of such an impairment, or being regarded as having such an impairment." Major life activities include being able to take care of one's self, being able to carry on a social life, being able to get an education, and being able to hold a job. It also means having access to transportation, recreational facilities, housing, and all public facilities.

But what's really behind that legal definition? What does having a disability mean for the 48 million Americans who live with a physical or learning disability? Sometimes it means discrimination, or being left out of recreational activities, or being unable to earn a living. Sometimes it means loneliness, low self-esteem, and being shut off from the world. A Lou Harris poll found that people with disabilities are "uniquely underprivileged," "poorer" than most of the American population, "less educated," and "have less of a social life." The Harris poll also found that discrimination denies people with disabilities the opportunities to compete on an equal basis with nondisabled people or to pursue all opportunities (see Williams and Nagle, "The ADA"). President George Bush, who signed the Americans with Disabilities Act into law in 1990, called people with disabilities "[the] largest minority in America."

Approximately two-thirds of the disabled Americans who are between the ages of 16 and 64 are unemployed. Sixty-six percent of working-age disabled individuals who are not employed say that they would like to find employment. Eighty-two percent of people with disabilities said they would be willing to give up government assistance in exchange for a full-time job. In real numbers, 8.5

million individuals who are disabled want to work but cannot find employment. But having a disability does not have to condemn anyone to becoming part of those statistics. With proper attitudes, environmental adjustments, and appropriate assistive technology, it could mean only that some people do things a little differently than others. Computers have done much to make work easier and less time consuming for everyone. Adaptive technology offers people with disabilities the opportunity not just to use computers, but to use computers to complete tasks that were previously not possible for them. The ability to use computers, software, adaptive technology, and electronic information gives people with disabilities the tools to go to school and to hold jobs.

Important Terms

Disability

Physical, emotional, or mental impairment that limits one or more of a person's major life activities. This includes impairments or limitations that are not visible. For example, a person with heart disease may have difficulty walking long distances and thus has a disability.

Hardware

Computers and the associated physical equipment involved in using computers. This includes printers, speech synthesizers, monitors, keyboards, and a long list of other equipment.

Software

Data—such as programs, routines, and symbolic languages—essential to the operation of computers.

Adaptive, Adapted, or Assistive Technology

Computer software and hardware that have been modified to be accessible by people with disabilities, or equipment that has been created to be compensatory tools for people with disabilities.

Computer Access Barriers

The various barriers to computer use that confront disabled individuals. For instance, a blind student can't see a computer screen, and a student without hand movement can't use a standard keyboard.

Compensatory Strategies

Computer use for tasks that are not normally done on the computer. A disabled student might use a computer to read books, conduct research, make notes, take exams, or communicate in class. A disabled student may not have any classes that normally require computer use, but the student might still use computers to participate fully in all of them.

Electronic Information

Includes material (such as books, journals, newspapers, and magazines) that is available in electronic formats, such as on floppy disks, CD-ROMs, and over the Internet.

Disabilities by Category

There are hundreds of different causes for each kind of disability that a person might have. Regardless of cause, disability types have been grouped into six broad categories for the purpose of identifying strategies to get past environmental barriers and to compensate for the difficulties caused by each disability. Thus, although one person may have no hand usage because of a stroke, and another person may have no hand usage because the hand was severed in an accident, both need computer input devices that do not rely on hand usage. For the purposes of this book, the *reason* a person has a disability rarely matters. Here, we are concerned only with the limitation that exists because of the disability. The following categories are used in this book:

- Vision impairments
- Mobility (orthopedic) impairments
- Hearing impairments
- Learning disabilities
- Speech impairments
- Traumatic brain injuries

Vision Impairments

This category includes people with low vision, functional vision, color blindness, and blindness. People with vision impairments have problems seeing computer screens and keyboards. They also have difficulty reading printed materials. Unfortunately, as computing software and information continues to lean more toward graphical user interfaces (GUI), additional barriers to computer use by people with vision impairments are being built in on standard systems.

Mobility Impairments

There are two groups in this category. The first involves people who use wheelchairs. For them, the important issue is making labs, classrooms, libraries, and other areas wheelchair accessible. The second group comprises people who have no hand usage and therefore are limited in using standard computer input and output devices. Both groups include people who have paralysis, missing limbs, and limited body control or body movement.

Hearing Impairments

This category includes people who are hard-of-hearing and people who are deaf. People with hearing impairments have little problem using standard computers. However, as computers and electronic information are increasingly designed to include more sound cues, there is the probability that access barriers for people with hearing impairments will be built into computing systems in the future.

Learning Disabilities

This category includes a range of disabilities from visual perception problems to aural processing difficulties. Although there are some learning disabilities that make it difficult for a person to use computers, the computing solutions suggested for people with learning disabilities generally tend to be compensatory.

Speech Impairments

In this category, which includes people who have limited, poor, or no speech, the main objective is to offer compensatory strategies that will help a speech-impaired individual communicate within a classroom or campus setting. Generally there are no barriers to using standard computing equipment.

Traumatic Brain Injuries

People with traumatic brain injury or damage may have one or more of the disabilities listed above. For example, a person may have poor vision (or no vision) due to a brain injury, limited or no mobility, speech difficulties, hearing loss, or learning disabilities. After the individual is assessed for his or her disabilities, it may be necessary to look for adaptive approaches in more than one category. In addition, there are certain problems—such as memory loss—that can also be helped through computing strategies such as computer alarm clocks or daily calendars.

THE MONEY QUESTION

What are the costs of making adaptive computing accommodations for students, faculty, and staff with disabilities? Does every disabled individual on your campus require a sophisticated system that costs thousands of dollars? Is exotic—and expensive—architecture, equipment, and technology required to give your students full access to your campus? Not necessarily. While it's true that some systems can cost thousands of dollars, most adaptive technologies are reasonably priced and add only moderately to the cost of regular computers and peripherals.

For example, Braille embossers can run as high as $37,000 for the Braille 200 Interpoint Printer—which produces 600 pages of 6- or 8-dot Braille per hour, and which will most likely *not* be found on a college campus—or as low as $3,800 for a model that is much slower and works with both Macintosh and IBM compatibles. Obviously, the better choice for a college campus trying to use resources wisely is the less sophisticated $3,800 model. With such a wide price range, the key is for each campus service provider to analyze the needs of the campus and to determine how to get the most useful technology for the dollar.

Digital Equipment Corporation produces DECtalk, a voice synthesis system that many say is the best on the market. It sells for about $1,200 for a single slot card for IBM PCs, or $4,500 as a VAX peripheral device. Vocal-Eyes, a screen reader for character-based applications on MS-DOS systems, goes for about $450, while Sounding Board LT provides speech synthesis through a hardware adapter for Toshiba laptops for around $400. Another popular workhorse is the JAWS screen reader, which works with most speech synthesizers and costs around $500. These useful applications would be reasonable in cost for most college and university campuses.

At the low end of the scale, there are many technologies that cost only a couple of hundred dollars (or less) and will improve access for many individuals for several years. Magic Keyboard is a $50 translation program that uses graphics to create large character sets for people with low vision. Another good program is Zoomer—around $150—a memory-resident screen enlargement program for IBM PT/XT/AT computers and true compatibles. An excellent system for people with hearing impairments is the H211 Conference Intertalk and H213 Expander for around $80.

And then there are the popular programs that don't cost a dime. KeyLock is a memory-resident program that changes the *Ctrl*, *Alt*, and left *Shift* keys into locking keys so that people with limited hand usage can type key sequences.

BENEFITS OF ADAPTIVE COMPUTING

The benefits of adaptive computing technology and support services for students with disabilities show up in higher grade point averages, students being able to take more classes per semester, a reduced probation and drop-out rate, and an increased likelihood of the students being able to pass their full class load. A study conducted at the University of Nebraska shows the benefits of adaptive technology on that campus (see Table 1.1).

TABLE 1.1

ACHIEVEMENT AND RETENTION BENEFITS STUDY, UNIVERSITY OF NEBRASKA, LINCOLN

	1985–86	1986–87	Percent Improvement
Average GPA	2.3	2.8	21%
Average Hours Passed	9.4	11.2	19%
Individuals on Probation	13.0	2.0	77%
Percentage Who Passed Full Class Load	44.8%	85%	90%
Students Served	29	20	

COMPUTERS AS PART OF THE U.S. INFRASTRUCTURE

In recent years, computer use has expanded from a few technical disciplines to almost every aspect of academic and administrative activity in education. The widespread integration of computing technology into postsecondary education—and our entire society—dictates the need to provide equal access to computing technology for all users, as well as compensatory strategies for people with disabilities.

Students today need access to a variety of computer hardware and software even before they graduate from high school, and as they enter higher education and then the workforce, the demand for computing skills and computer literacy becomes even greater. Colleges and universities must plan and implement the technology, procedures, and services that will provide all students with equitable and reasonable computing access, as well as compensatory strategies.

Specifically, service providers on college and university campuses should examine computing services provided for the general campus population and make sure that appropriate equivalent services are provided for students, faculty, and staff members with disabilities. In particular, equivalence should be ensured in these areas:

- Access to general computing sites and general computing consultation
- Opportunity to benefit from computer resale programs (offer adaptive equipment when possible)
- Access to technical support and repair services
- Access to discipline-specific and instructional software

PROVIDING ADAPTIVE COMPUTER TECHNOLOGY ON CAMPUS

There are four broad service areas to consider when providing adaptive computer technology on college and university campuses—academic computing centers, discipline-specific computing, print and online services, and computer hardware and software as compensatory tools.

Academic Computing Centers

All academic computing centers must provide full wheelchair accessibility. Additionally, individual workstations that present barriers of various kinds to people with disabilities can be made accessible through the use of accommodations such as adjustable tables, special keyboards, and monitor stands (see Chapter 5). Computing centers can begin to improve access for a wide range of users by making basic modifications, most of which have low start-up costs. More specialized accommodations can be made in response to demand and the anticipated needs of the future disabled population.

Campuses should pay particular attention to the flexibility of the adaptive computer systems they establish in general computing facilities. Ideally, adaptive systems should accommodate the abilities and preferences of several users.

Discipline-Specific Computing

Discipline-specific and instructional support services include computing activities as basic as writing freshman compositions and as sophisticated as using computer-aided engineering design programs or gaining access to online legal reference materials. As adaptive computing for users with disabilities is increasingly integrated into discipline-specific computing subjects, students, faculty, and staff will require greater levels of support. Necessary services might include adapting course-specific hardware and software, training faculty and staff in particular disciplines to use and work with adaptive technology, and identifying and developing accessible courseware.

Print and Online Services

Students with disabilities must also have full access to research sources such as online library catalogs and CD-ROMs that offer encyclopedias, journals, and dissertation abstracts. Online computing services can be useful both for making campus computing resources accessible and as compensatory strategies. Online information offers one of the greatest opportunities for participation in academic life for people who have difficulty using traditional texts. For example, those who have never been able to read a course catalog in print may be able to do so if it is available online.

Electronic campuswide information services may offer online information such as the schedule of campus events, campus job listings, financial aid information, and listings of extracurricular activities. If so, the campus must make arrangements for adaptive strategies that will allow all students to have access to such information.

Compensatory Tools

Compensatory tools are computing hardware and software that can be used for tasks not normally accomplished on a computer. These tasks include reading, writing, and organizing information. Students with disabilities may encounter difficulty in any one of these areas, or a combination of them. Compensatory computer technology can help many students be more independent. In the classroom, this might include computerized assistance in reading, note taking, and exam taking. Outside the classroom, this might include computerized support for both home and lab assignments.

Some issues that may arise when planning compensatory strategies for disabled students include the availability of portable equipment and the provision of duplicate equipment for home and campus use. In addition, some professors balk at having students use computers to take notes in class or to take exams. It is the responsibility of disabled student service providers to work with professors who have concerns about the use of such aids.

General Support

In addition to adaptive technology for academic computing centers, discipline-specific computing, accessing print and online services, and compensatory purposes, the following additional general services should be provided by the appropriate campus departments for students with disabilities:

- Telephone registration should be supplemented with a telecommunication device for deaf and hard-of-hearing individuals (TTY) or some equally appropriate means of access for people with hearing impairments.
- Catalogs and schedules should be made available in an accessible format—Braille, large print, audiotape, or electronic format—for students who have vision impairments.

Other support services also should be developed and implemented:

- Training and consulting on adaptive devices and standard equipment should be provided both for individuals and for campus departments.
- Disabled students, faculty, staff, and department representatives should be consulted about appropriate adaptive equipment.

- Practical applications of adaptive technology geared to the campus educational and computing environment should be researched, developed, and evaluated.
- Alternative documentation must be provided for adaptive technology training, usage, and maintenance.

WHERE ARE WE HEADING?

When computing services are provided to the general campus population or are required for coursework, degree completion, or campus employment, equipment and services must be in place to accommodate everyone. Campus computing services should enlist the support of disabled student service offices and disabled student organizations to understand the needs of students with disabilities. And disabled student services program personnel should consult with campus computing services for help in understanding computing issues and the possibilities that are offered through adaptive technology.

Twenty years ago, less than 500,000 disabled students were able to get the public education promised to them. Today that number exceeds 4.5 million. Approximately 180,000 students with disabilities graduate from high school each year. While those numbers reflect improvement, they highlight the fact that our education system still has a great deal of work to do. With planning and the effective use of technology, institutions of higher education can help provide equal education to all students. At the same time, colleges and universities can prepare those students to take their places in the workforce and in society.

In the business world, employers are beginning to regard computing ability as a basic skill required of all new employees. Indeed, computer technology makes things easier for most people, and for a person with a disability, that same technology makes many ordinary tasks possible for the first time. Adaptive computer technology, combined with nonelectronic aids and appropriate human interaction, can provide a means for people with disabilities to do most of the same jobs as nondisabled people.

Now that we've explained why adaptive computing systems are important, we will discuss some of the associated technology, the services necessary to support that technology, and how to determine what resources are necessary to provide services. We'll consider computers as compensatory tools; different computer access strategies that will help accommodate people with various functional limitations; how to provide an accessible environment; the training, consulting, and technical support necessary to provide services; and strategies to provide appropriate staffing, fulfill equipment needs, and establish funding.

It's not enough that adaptive computer technology exists. The challenge is to stay informed about new developments and to make sure that adaptive computer technology and information about it is available to everyone.

CHAPTER 2

The Americans with Disabilities Act of 1990

By now, everybody in the United States has heard about the Americans with Disabilities Act of 1990 (ADA). Some see it as a keystone document that will lead to the emancipation and liberation of all people with disabilities. Others regard it as just one more piece of legislation that will result in an avalanche of lawsuits, require huge amounts of paperwork, and generally be a costly roadblock to getting anything accomplished. There is some truth in both of these views.

HISTORY OF DISABILITY LAW

Disability legislation has been around for some time, especially in the area of higher education. The ADA is the latest—and by far the most wide reaching—of a whole string of federal mandates, starting with the Architectural Barriers Act of 1968. Although it did not apply directly to educational facilities, the 1968 act required federal facilities to remove architectural barriers by providing such things as ramps, elevators, and other amenities that would allow access to buildings by people with disabilities.

The Architectural Barriers Act was followed by the Rehabilitation Act of 1973, which incorporated the standards of the earlier law and added provisions that forbade discrimination on the basis of disability in any program receiving or benefiting from federal aid. Sections 503 and 504 of the Rehabilitation Act were aimed specifically at education. Those sections required that all educational programs and all campus employment be accessible to students, teachers, and campus employees with disabilities.

Then came the computer revolution. As campuses across the nation began to computerize their operations, it became apparent that computers must also be accessible to people with disabilities. In 1986, Congress amended the Rehabilitation Act. Section 508 of that amendment—commonly known as the "electronic curb cuts" legislation—mandated that all electronic office equipment and computers used in any federally funded programs be accessible.

Section 508 of the Rehabilitation Act was further amended in 1992. The section (referred to as Section 509 in the 1992 amendment) mandated that the secretary, through the director of the National Institute on Disability and Rehabilitation Research (NIDRR), and the administrator of the General Services Administration must work with the electronics and information technology industry to develop guidelines for federal agencies that would ensure that electronic and information technology accessibility is usable and accessible to people with disabilities. The section specifically includes all media.

In 1988, Congress passed the Technology-Related Assistance for Individuals with Disabilities Act (the Tech Act). This legislation provided funding for state programs to increase awareness of the need for assistive technology, educate people about it, and help make it more available. All 50 states have qualified for such funding (see Appendix B for the RESNA office, which can refer you to the Tech Act office in your state).

The Americans with Disabilities Act, passed in 1990, went into effect in 1992. It is a logical evolution and marriage of two legislative movements. The first is the movement to provide access for people with disabilities to mainstream education, employment, and recreation. The ADA generally takes the provisions of these previous disability-access laws, updates them, and extends them beyond federally funded institutions to all of society. Where the earlier laws prohibited discrimination, the ADA mandates an affirmative obligation to make reasonable efforts to accommodate the needs of people with disabilities and to help them overcome barriers to success.

The second legislative movement on which the ADA was based is the ongoing effort in the United States to recognize and enforce civil rights. Disability law is civil rights law. The ADA provides similar wording, penalties, and obligations as earlier civil rights legislation, such as laws that ban discrimination against women and against racial and ethnic groups.

Colleges and universities that were in compliance with the previous legislation pertaining to people with disabilities—specifically, Section 504, which adopted standards from the Architectural Barriers Act—were far ahead of private businesses and other institutions who began compliance efforts with the passage of the ADA. Institutions that had failed to abide by the strictures of the Architectural Barriers Act of 1968 faced the costly task of retrofitting their buildings to include such features as automatic doors and elevators. Even today, many institutions—struggling to fulfill their educational mandates in an era of ever-tightening budgets—continue to lag behind in their compliance with the ADA legislation. But they need to exercise care in where they choose to economize.

Colleges and universities play a crucial role in preparing people to take their place in the workplace and society. As such, those institutions are on the front lines of the legal battlefield on which the ultimate boundaries and parameters of the ADA are being tested and determined. How they emerge from those battles and at what cost will depend in large part on the decisions they make along the way.

THE MANDATE FOR "REASONABLE ACCOMMODATIONS"

The ADA requires that "reasonable accommodations" be made to provide access for people with disabilities. What does this mean? There are guidelines available, but their interpretation will be made in court, on a case-by-case basis (see the last section in this chapter for how to obtain illustrative settlement agreements).

Some things, however, are clear. According to the law, people are considered to have disabilities if they have a physical or mental condition that substantially limits one or more of their major life activities, a record of such an impairment, or the perception by others that they are impaired. That covers not just people who have a problem seeing, hearing, speaking, walking, breathing, learning, or caring for themselves, but also people who have had such problems in the past—such as people with histories of mental illness or recovered alcoholics. It also applies to people who are regarded and treated as if they were disabled, even though they may not be; for example, a person who has a severe disfigurement.

The ADA does not mandate that unqualified individuals with disabilities be admitted as students or hired as employees. But if a candidate is otherwise qualified and can perform the essential tasks required, reasonable accommodations must be made available. Colleges and universities are required to have a compliance officer on staff to make sure the provisions of the ADA are being carried out.

CAMPUS SELF-EVALUATION

Every public college and university is required to conduct a self-evaluation of the services it offers in every department to make sure those services are accessible to disabled people. This self-evaluation is more than just paperwork. It documents in black and white what the needs of a campus are and what resources are available on campus to fill those needs. It shows where a campus is weak and highlights areas of potential problems. It places the campus on the road to compliance and shows it which direction to take.

One element of the self-evaluation is an assessment of user needs. How many disabled students are on campus, what are their disabilities, and what are their areas of study? This assessment may be more difficult to complete than it first appears, since it is illegal to require people to report whether or not they are disabled. The most reasonable approach is a voluntary survey form given to all students in which they may disclose their special needs. This gives administrators a target population and helps them determine which needs to address first.

When it comes to computer accessibility, colleges and universities need to consider four broad questions in their self-evaluation:

- How accessible are the buildings and rooms where the computers are located?
- What problems will disabled students face putting information into a computer?
- What problems will they have getting output from a computer?
- Are all training materials and documentation accessible to students with vision, hearing, learning, and mobility impairments?

For instance, some students with mobility impairments may have difficulty using a keyboard. They may need headwands to push the keys or perhaps a sticky-key program that allows a sequence of keystrokes—such as *Ctrl*, then *Q*—to be interpreted as depressing both keys simultaneously. Or they may need an alternative method for handling and loading CD-ROMs or floppy disks. Vision-impaired people may be able to use a keyboard but unable to read the screen. They may need a program that magnifies the words or even a speech synthesizer that can read the words to them. Documentation—such as lab procedures and regulations, hardware configuration information, and software manuals—must be provided in alternative formats for students with disabilities. And none of the computer adaptations will mean anything if disabled people are not able to gain physical access to the room in which the computer is placed.

A self-evaluation will not protect a campus from lawsuits, but it can be used as evidence of effort to comply with ADA in the unfortunate event that demonstrating such an effort becomes necessary. A well-conducted self-evaluation of all departments and labs that include computers can also be used to determine what your campus needs. Armed with a self-evaluation, the college or university will be able to plan for the future and show that it is making an effort to address possible shortcomings. Both benefits are important.

BE PROACTIVE

The key to dealing with the ADA is to be proactive. Institutions that failed to anticipate the architectural standards of the Rehabilitation Act of 1973 had to spend even more money retrofitting recently built campus buildings. Similarly, the institutions of today that fail to heed the increasing demands for accessibility are likely to pay dearly. The lesson is to look ahead and plan.

It may not be easy. Although the ADA mandates reasonable accommodations, it does not specify exactly what "reasonable" means. By looking at past decisions it is possible to get an idea of what types of accommodations might be deemed reasonable in court.

Take the case of a private, west coast university that serves about 3,500 students. In 1991, an 18-year-old blind woman, referred to only as M in government documents, enrolled as a student. Prior to her enrollment, she asked the university to provide her with several types of equipment to assist her in her classes, additional time to take examinations, and note-taking equipment. The university's coordinator of disabled student services sent a form to her professors notifying them of her request, but the university did not provide any of the required equipment. Her father, however, bought her a Braille'n'Speak, a personal computer with a speech synthesizer, and a Braille scanner and printer.

Before her first classes began, she wrote a letter to the college in which she again made several requests: (1) that the university provide her with double the number of tutor hours available for nondisabled students; (2) that she be provided twice the time for taking tests that nondisabled students had; (3) that test materials be in a form in which she could check her answers before turning in the test; and (4) that she be allowed to tape-record lectures.

In response, the university's disabled student services coordinator and the director of the learning resource center suggested that she ask a classmate for assistance with notes and seek the help of campus tutors. When she visited the campus bookstore to buy her textbooks, she found only 1 of her 12 textbooks was in a form she could use; it was on audiotape. Again, she and her father appealed to the university to provide her with the proper equipment and assistance to allow her access to her courses.

The university sent each of her professors a notice that M would be one of their students and would need assistance in two ways—a fellow classmate to take notes and additional time for tests. She was also given permission to tape-record lectures and discussions, but the university did not supply her with a tape recorder or tapes. And it did nothing to inform her during lectures about information provided on the blackboard or in any other visual form. She had to wait until after the lecture for her reader's description.

The U.S. Department of Education's Office for Civil Rights found that the university had failed to provide adequate accessibility for M in several areas. The university was required either to provide M with equipment to take her own notes or to provide the notes taken by her classmate in a directly usable form such as Braille. It also had to inform her about what was on the blackboard during the lecture. That meant the professor had to briefly describe what was on the blackboard and give her copy of the blackboard information in a usable form.

Although the university did give M more time to take tests, the government took issue with the way the university administered those tests. For essay questions, the professor would read the question to M, who would then compose an answer on her computer. If the test required only brief answers to questions, the professor would read each question to her and she would respond with the answer. That may seem fairly clear-cut, but the government ruled that taking a test in a one-on-one setting with the professor who will be giving the grade introduced an element of stress exceeding that experienced by the rest of the students. It also denied M the opportunity to review her answers before submitting the test and the opportunity to select the order in which she answered the questions. The university was required to provide M with a copy of the test in an accessible form that would allow her to take it under conditions equivalent to those afforded her classmates. It also had to give her an accessible copy of the graded test and her answers if the other students got their tests back.

The government also found that none of the computers the college provided for student use were accessible to blind students. It required that the college equip at least one computer with adaptive software and equipment to make it accessible to blind students and that the adapted equipment be available during the same hours and conditions as the computers for nondisabled students. Both textbooks and handouts would have to be made accessible— either in Braille or on audiotape. Just providing a reader to read the text to the student was not sufficient.

The ruling was a compromise negotiated between the university and the government. In the end, the university made the required accommodations, and M proceeded with her education.

There are many gray areas, however, and many questions that remain unanswered. A legal review of the ADA compliance at one small college gives the example of an English composition class: Providing a disabled student with a laptop computer, having a scribe to write down what the student dictates, and allowing more time for the student to take tests would all probably be considered reasonable accommodations. Exempting the student from the requirement to produce coherent sentences, on the other hand, would go beyond a reasonable accommodation. Student use of computer spelling checkers or grammar checkers to correct errors before turning in a test paper was a gray area. Grayer still are distinctions between disability categories. While it might be appropriate for a student with a learning disability to use a spelling checker, it might not be appropriate for a student with a mobility disability.

SIZE COUNTS

What is reasonable for one institution may not be for another. A tiny college of less than 1,000 students is not held to the same standard as a huge state university with, perhaps, more than 30 times that enrollment and vastly superior resources. But are there any limits to how far an institution need go to accommodate students and staff who are disabled? When a very large university has a yearly budget of as much as $1 billion, is there any accommodation that is truly unreasonable? And just how wide a population will be entitled to the protection of the disability umbrella? The goal for your university or college should be to have other universities and colleges be the ones forced to find out the answers to such questions in court. That goal can best be realized by responding to the needs of the disabled students, teachers, and campus employees and by taking whatever steps are necessary to resolve potential conflicts before they become litigation.

LIBERATION FOR ALL?

Will the ADA result in the emancipation and liberation of all people with disabilities? It will certainly help. It will clear away many of the barriers that keep people with disabilities from full participation in work and other aspects of community life. Of course, it cannot mandate that disabled people take advantage of these new opportunities, nor can it remove all the barriers they face. Some individuals with disabilities may decide that it is too difficult to find reliable transportation to the job site. Others may be afraid of losing government-provided medical benefits if they accept employment. And some barriers are inherent in the disability itself—the ADA will not make it possible for blind people to see or for people with speech impairments to speak. But the ADA will open the door to education, employment, recreation, and every other aspect of society. Many will pass through that door, others will not.

Will the ADA result in costly lawsuits, require paperwork, and impede the ability of a business or institution to accomplish its goals? To greater and lesser extents, it almost certainly will. People will sue. Some of the litigation will be frivolous; most will not. Paperwork will be required, both to document an institution's compliance and to protect the institution in case of a problem. And at times, it will be an impediment. If a college or university has to devote more time or resources to a handful of disabled students, there will be less time and resources available for the rest of the student body.

In the end, however, a whole class of people will gain admittance to the mainstream of society. People once dependent on the government will become self-sufficient. Society and business will profit from the contributions of people previously denied the opportunity to contribute. Will it be worth it? The answer is an unqualified "yes."

ADDITIONAL INFORMATION ON THE ADA

ADA Legal Documents and Settlement Agreements

For copies of legal documents and illustrative settlement agreements, write to:

Freedom of Information/Privacy Act Branch
Administrative Management Section
Civil Rights Division
U.S. Department of Justice
P.O. Box 65310
Washington, DC 20035-5310
Fax: 202-514-6195

ADA Title I, Employment Provisions

The Equal Employment Opportunity Commission offers technical assistance to the public concerning Title I of the ADA.

- To order documents, call 800-669-3362 or 800-800-3302 (TTY).
- To ask questions, call 800-669-4000 or 800-669-6820 (TTY).

ADA Titles II and III, Public Transportation Provisions

The U.S. Department of Transportation offers technical assistance to the public concerning the public transportation provisions of Title II and Title III of the ADA.

- For ADA documents and general questions, call 202-366-1656 or 202-366-4567 (TTY).
- For ADA legal questions, call 202-366-1936 (has relay service).
- For information on complaints and enforcement, call 202-366-2285 or 202-366-0153 (TTY).

ADA Title IV

The Federal Communications Commission offers technical assistance to the public concerning Title IV of the ADA.

- To request ADA documents and ask general questions, call 202-418-0190 or 202-418-2555 (TTY).

- To ask ADA legal questions, call 202-634-1798 or 202-418-0484 (TTY).
- For information on complaints and enforcement, call: 202-632-7553 or 202-418-0485 (TTY).

Accessibility Guidelines

The U.S. Architectural and Transportation Barriers Compliance Board, or Access Board, offers technical assistance to the public on the ADA Accessibility Guidelines.

- For ADA documents and questions, call 800-872-2253 or 800-993-2822 (TTY).

Regional Centers for Technical Assistance

The National Institute on Disability and Rehabilitation Research (NIDRR) of the U.S. Department of Education has funded 10 regional centers to provide technical assistance on the ADA.

- For information, call 800-949-4232 (voice and TTY; your call will automatically connect to the closest center).

Reasonable Accommodation in the Workplace

The Job Accommodation Network (JAN) is a free telephone consulting service funded by the President's Committee on Employment of People with Disabilities. It provides information and advice to employers and people with disabilities on reasonable accommodation in the workplace.

- For information on accommodations in the workplace, call 800-526-7234 (voice and TTY).

WHERE TO FILE COMPLAINTS

Title I

Complaints about violations of Title I (employment) by units of state and local government or by private employers should be filed with the Equal Employment Opportunity Commission. Call 800-669-4000 or 800-669-6820 (TTY) for the field office in your area.

Titles II and III

Complaints about violations of Title II by units of state and local government or violations of Title III by public accommodations and commercial facilities should be filed with the following office:

U.S. Department of Justice
Civil Rights Division
Disability Rights Section
P.O. Box 66738
Washington, DC 20035-6738

CHAPTER 3

Planning an
Adaptive Computing Program

T he introduction of computers and computer technology into our education system has greatly enhanced learning. Access to computers is valuable for study and research, and it also permits students to acquire computer skills that will be valuable in employment settings. Adaptive computing technology and support services have been of enormous benefit to students with disabilities.

Computer technology also makes it possible for most people with disabilities to enroll in school and participate fully as students. Further, technology and support services help ensure that disabled students stay in school and achieve academic success. Through adaptive computing technology, students with disabilities can become more self-reliant in their coursework, in research, and in pursuing employment opportunities.

What is the best way to plan and implement adaptive technology and support services that will benefit the greatest number of people on your campus? There are several philosophies on how to establish such services, but some basic steps are applicable regardless of the particular approach.

STEP ONE: DEVELOP A TASK FORCE

Develop a task force committed to establishing adaptive computing technology and support services on your campus. When creating a task force, include key people and groups. There may be many organizational boundaries to cross, especially on larger campuses. The success of your program will depend on getting the necessary commitment from various departments, including university administration, disabled student services, academic computing, campus libraries, and the 504-ADA compliance office (many schools have established an office to ensure that the campus meets both ADA and Section 504 accessibility requirements).

To develop an effective task force, ask these questions: Who are the key people on campus who must say "yes" before a disability support program can be implemented, and how can their ideas be incorporated into your plan? How many people should be on the advisory team, and from which parts of the college or university should they come?

As you establish the task force, initiate a dialogue among members by asking them to consider these questions: How can potential service providers persuade the school's administrators to support adaptive computer technology services? Once an initial commitment is made, how can the school administrators be convinced to provide permanent staff and resources? How do administrators determine who should be responsible for the program? What is the minimum your school must do to meet the requirements in disability-access legislation and standards? How can your school become proactive in its efforts to comply with the law? How should a director of disabled student services promote an adaptive computing technology program so as not to neglect other disabled student services? How can funding be obtained for a new program? What role should the director of academic computing services play in establishing adaptive computing technology within the campus computing environment? Whose responsibility is it to integrate this technology into an increasingly distributed campus computing infrastructure? What role can students and staff play in establishing adaptive computer technology on your campus, and how can they make their preferences known? How can each task force member contribute to the overall effort?

Regardless of the fields from which the people on the task force come, there are specific actions they can take to ensure that the most effective program will be established—both in terms of serving students and complying with the law. To do this, it is important to build program support at the highest level. This may necessitate recognizing that you personally may not be in the political or organizational position to approach high-level administrators such as the president or chancellor of the university.

Start your task force by identifying possible supporters. Consider enlisting the aid of sympathetic administrators and faculty, including those with disabilities. Involve students or disabled-student organizations that recognize the need for adaptive technology and support services—and who might demand services if they are not provided or if they are taken away. Establish a campus disability advisory committee that will help lobby for services. Try to enlist the aid of community organizations such as the department of rehabilitation and centers of independent living (places where people with one or more severe disabilities go to learn independent living skills). Launch a campus publicity campaign to bring the needs of students with disabilities to the attention of the entire student body. Give equipment demonstrations whenever possible—seeing students use adapted computing equipment persuades many administrators.

Be sure to have the task force establish goals for both current and future needs. As you get commitments of initial support and address the immediate need for accessible computing equipment and services, make sure that you also get a pledge for the long-term support of your proposed program.

Particular questions should be considered by the task force:

- Who are your clients—students? faculty and staff? departments and labs?
- What are your clients' needs?
- What people, resources, and funds are required to meet your clients' needs, both today and in the future?
- Where should services be provided?
- How can your program receive administration support and resources?
- Who will be responsible for the program?

Identify who must ultimately approve the task force's proposal, and decide what type of document or justification will be required to secure an agreement to implement a support program.

STEP TWO: ASSESS THE NEED

Every program must begin with a careful assessment of the current needs of the school, students, faculty, and staff, as well as a projection of future trends. Before equipment is purchased and services are implemented, it is important to know who will be using the equipment and services, both now and in the future.

How Many Students and Staff with Disabilities Are Currently on Campus?

An office for disabled student services (or a similar office) may have this information. Such offices sometimes have records on students and staff who have requested services, and they may also know of students and staff whose disabilities are most easily identified—those who use wheelchairs, service dogs, crutches, or some other obvious accommodation.

Students and staff with hearing, speech, or learning disabilities; traumatic brain damage; epilepsy; attention deficit disorder; or other less visible disabilities may be harder to identify. In fact, some students and staff members may have chosen not to identify themselves to campus administrators or personnel.

Other individuals with disabilities may not know that services are available and may have become self-sufficient in their daily activities. Even so, these students might benefit from the services you will provide. You may also need to provide services to students and staff with temporary disabilities.

What Types of Disabilities
Do Current Students and Staff Have?

The answer to this question will help determine what type of equipment is most practical, given the demographics of your particular campus. For some individuals with disabilities, no special accommodations are required for computer access—standard equipment will meet their needs. For other students and staff members, a minimum of accommodation is necessary. And for some students and staff members, the services provided will determine whether or not they can complete their courses of study or perform their jobs. For a number of reasons, some college and university campuses draw people with specific types of disabilities more than others. It is worth the effort for you to consider the demographics of your disabled student and staff population and use that information to help determine how you should spend your budget. Although every campus should be able to accommodate students and staff with any kind of disability, you may find, for example, that you have a much larger number of blind students than deaf students, so you will want to spend more of your budget on equipment for people with vision impairments.

Also consider the types of adaptive equipment that will be necessary to provide compensatory tools for students and staff with disabilities. Compensatory systems will include computer hardware and software that help disabled students perform tasks more easily, such as spelling checkers for students with learning disabilities or abbreviation expansion for people with mobility impairments. See Chapter 7 for more information on compensatory tools and strategies.

What Courses and Disciplines Are Using Computing as
Part of Their Regular Coursework?

As computers have become more commonplace, they are being used not only in science, engineering, and mathematics, but also in general education courses. Everything from freshman composition to American history is being taught using computers. Identify what courses require computer use to help determine what type of equipment—and what amount and configurations—will be necessary to support your students with disabilities. Also consider what type of adaptive equipment will be necessary to provide compensatory tools for students and staff with disabilities.

What Computing Services Are Available for Your General Campus Population?

Does your campus use IBM and IBM-compatible equipment, Macintosh equipment, advanced workstations, or local area networks? Every system in use on your campus must be made available and accessible to your disabled students. What general computing lab services are available on your campus? You must ensure that adaptive labs and adaptive workstations are available during the same hours as general labs. Also, be sure to look at your campus libraries. They, too, must be both physically and informationally accessible to all students and staff members.

What Computing Access or Services Already Exist on Campus?

When you plan for the future, the first place to look is to the past. What accommodations has your campus already provided for students with disabilities? Examine what is in place, and build on that. By doing so, you will be able to provide the most cost-efficient system. And because you will be building on a program that is already in place, you can make an analysis to determine the gaps in your existing system, then fill them at the same time that you acquire equipment to serve future students and staff members.

What Do Disabled Students and Staff Members Have to Say?

Many times when bureaucracies set out to meet the needs of a specific population, they make one critical error: they do studies, they find facts, they analyze—but they forget to talk to the people they're trying to serve. This has resulted in ramps that are too steep for a person in a wheelchair to navigate and doors that are too heavy for some individuals to open. Find out from your staff and students what specific adaptive devices and accommodations are being used today by persons who are disabled. Build a list of these accommodations both for today and for future reference and use.

The numbers and information that you compile through an "immediate needs" checklist will give a rough representation of what your campus needs today, and consumer input from students with disabilities can also help guide program development. Remember that the degree of input is directly related to how aware potential consumers are of the existence of a program. Many of your staff and students with disabilities may not know what adaptive computer technology can offer them, or of the technology available to meet their needs. It is important, therefore, to launch an awareness campaign along with any adaptive technology program.

Assessment Kit

EASI (Equal Access to Software and Information) has created a kit that helps colleges and universities get started on making an in-depth assessment of what equipment and services will best serve their disabled student and staff populations. The following material—from EASI's Adaptive Computing Evaluation Kit for Colleges and Universities—gives an idea on how to assess your campus needs. (The EASI kit is available, for a fee, through the EASI; see Appendix B for contact information.)

EASI suggests that service providers give a survey worksheet to every disabled individual on campus. The survey responses will help determine the best course for your campus, including what will be needed in the way of equipment, facility, staffing, and training.

The first portion of the worksheet should explain that the survey is being conducted to help determine the needs of students, faculty, staff, and others who use computers in each department on campus. The survey should ask the respondent to identify himself or herself as a member of the student body, faculty, or staff, or an individual from the general public who has computing privileges on campus. It should then ask the respondent to indicate the categories in which he or she has disability and to describe the severity of disability as either mild, moderate, or severe. The categories should include vision impaired/blind, hearing impaired/deaf, mobility impaired, learning disabled, traumatic brain injured, and speech impaired.

Next, the respondent should be asked to describe experiences with campus computing. Specifically, determine whether or not the person has used computers on campus, if there were problems trying to use computers on campus, and if help was offered. The respondent should describe what computer facilities were used, including department, building, and room.

Finally, the respondent should identify reasons for using the computer and whether or not the computer use was required for coursework. Reasons to use computers might include word processing, keeping business records, data storage and retrieval, course registration, teaching, student coursework, or research. The information from this kind of survey will help the task force identify the immediate needs of the campus.

STEP THREE: DEVELOP A LONG-RANGE PLAN

Long-range planning depends on looking at future growth trends. Of course, there is no crystal ball that will allow you gaze into the future to see what specific things students or staff members will require, but service providers can estimate future needs based on new technologies and other predictors. One area to consider when establishing services is the probable change in disability demographics that will accompany new computer access support services. For example, more children with severe disabilities are currently being integrated into the schools—from kindergarten through 12th grade—thanks to medical and technological advances and to opportunities created by legislation such as the Education for All Handicapped Children Act of 1975. Many of these students will eventually make their ways into the college system, and it is important to anticipate their needs when planning for future adaptive computing technology services.

As your task force develops long-range plans, remember that adapted equipment for students with disabilities must be equal to what is being supplied for the entire campus, and it must also be compatible with systems that are generally available. As part of your planning for the future, always keep in mind that campus adaptive computing technology support services should be prepared to serve people with all types of disabilities. Make sure you carefully examine what's on the horizon for your campus as you make purchases and implement programs. Be sure to consider the following issues:

- K–12 feeder schools and community colleges can help you forecast future needs. Build relationships with the schools that normally send students to your campus. Make them aware of your support capabilities and get from them a projection of how many students with college potential will be enrolling in your institution in the next three or four years. Offer a visitation program for their students with disabilities.
- More people with severe disabilities are now able to attend school and enter the workplace, thanks to new medical and technological advances. Through your relationship with the K–12 feeder schools, your state board of education, and the state division of rehabilitation services (DRS), you can attract people who never before considered college. Make them aware of the new kinds of medical and adaptive computing technology and its potential to facilitate their success in school and at work.
- Laws and legal mandates will continue to change. It is important to be familiar with relevant disability laws and what they require in the way of support and services.
- Older, "nontraditional" students are likely to play a significant role in your local enrollment population. Our society is moving from a manufacturing-based economy to an information-based economy. This places a premium on literacy, reading skills, and math. You can support disabled students and staff in these fields through the use of computer adaptations. You may find that the DRS will require people who have sustained disabling injuries to get training and make new career choices. These individuals are candidates for your program, and you should plan to meet their needs.

- People with less interest in degrees and more interest in skill development are increasingly attending college. Expect people who have disabilities to ask for specific courses that will improve their employment opportunities. Requested courses may include word processing, secretarial skills, and computer programming—courses that train individuals for the workplace. Work with the appropriate departments in your institution to provide computer adaptations for these courses. This is particularly important at community colleges.

STEP FOUR: CONSIDER TECHNOLOGY TRENDS

Technology trends are important to consider when first establishing services. Be prepared for rapid changes, especially in the field of computers and electronic information. Because adaptive computing technology changes so quickly, it is not uncommon to buy into one system and then see something better become available a short time later. Keep in mind that your campus will never have in place all the technology it needs. People change. Technology changes. Stay informed about the new technology on the market and what technology is best suited for particular students and staff.

It is important to balance student and staff needs with evolving adaptive computing technology. Get your campus on the notification lists of organizations that develop new products for people who are disabled. Volunteer to be a field-test site for new products. Subscribe to papers, magazines, and Internet mailing lists or discussion groups that carry disability technology information. (See Chapter 11 and Appendix C for contact information.)

Also, be careful as you choose equipment to ensure that your equipment and technology will work together. One of the most difficult challenges for adaptive technology service providers is making sure that an adaptive package works with the software and hardware of any particular system and doesn't "crash" it. Adaptive technicians spend a great deal of time working with systems to make them compatible. Enlist the aid of other adaptive tech labs for their recommendations.

STEP FIVE: WORK TO ENSURE EQUAL ACCESS

To ensure that they are not discriminating, campuses are morally and legally bound to provide computing access and services to disabled students at a level that is comparable to the general computing services. Thus, the need for adaptive computing services is directly related to the magnitude of general computing activities on your campus. General computing services may include computing lab access, library access, field support and repair, training, providing documentation, hardware consultation, and software consultation.

STEP SIX: FOCUS ON LEGAL RESPONSIBILITIES

It is crucial to make high-level administrators aware of their legal responsibility to provide adaptive computing technology services for students and staff with disabilities. In many cases, awareness of legal and social responsibilities comes from a new student whose adapted computer needs were met in elementary and high school. Sometimes it comes from an advocate—an administrator, staff member, or faculty member who is familiar with the field of adaptive computing technology and understands the need for services on every higher-education campus. Sometimes the awareness, and subsequently the services, have come from potential or actual legal action (see Chapter 2).

STEP SEVEN: BECOME ADVOCATES

By taking on the challenge of participation, task force members become advocates for setting up adaptive computer services on your campus. Once the task force members have become aware of the reasons for providing services and the benefits that will come from those services, it becomes the group's charge to spread the word and to promote the establishment of the best possible service system. As advocates, task force members have the duty of staying the course—getting other people involved, working with the students and staff, and setting up the equipment. Most importantly, the task force has the duty of keeping the university on track when it comes to complying fully with the law.

CHAPTER

Implementing an Adaptive Computing Program

I n this chapter, we focus on a series of strategies that will help you implement the program that you learned how to plan in Chapter 3. We first discuss implementation strategies and then outline the components of an implementation proposal that you can present to your school administration. After your task force or other work group has reached a consensus on the adaptive computing technology equipment, support, and services that should be established, there are several development strategies that can be used to get—and keep—the program approved and funded.

STRATEGY ONE: ESTABLISH THE PROGRAM

Create a pilot program to show the need for adaptive technology services and to demonstrate how the program will be run. Suggest a phased implementation plan that will establish services in increments over an agreed-on period. When you do this, be sure to lay the groundwork for establishing permanent program status, and include provisions for acquiring staff and equipment.

STRATEGY TWO: HOUSE THE PROGRAM

When adaptive computing technology services are first established, your campus will have to determine where to locate the physical and administrative home of the program. The key to setting up the most effective services is to be flexible and to adapt to the special requirements and restrictions of your campus. Your institution will need to determine who will administer the adaptive computing services program and how those services will be integrated on the campus. Your adaptive computer support services might be established as part of the disabled student services program, the academic computing services program, or the library.

All three entities offer important advantages and disadvantages for an adaptive technology program. Professionals working in a disabled student services office generally have the knowledge and expertise for meeting the special needs of individuals with disabilities. On the other hand, people working in disabled student services offices may not have enough technical computer experience to set up and administer adaptive computing services. Centers for academic computing services offer the computing infrastructure necessary for adaptive computing and also have staff members who have a great deal of technical expertise with computers, but they generally have little experience in working with individuals who have disabilities. Library services staff generally have access to online and print information, and making libraries accessible is a vital part of providing equal educational opportunity and access. Campus libraries are increasingly important players in computer support services for students with disabilities. Libraries and library support services can, and should, be partners with disabled student services and academic computing services in the overall campus implementation strategy.

Ideally, disabled student services, academic computing services, and library support services will work together to provide the best possible adaptive computing technology and support services. It may, however, make sense to choose one office as the primary program administrator.

Physical Home Base of the Program

The physical home base of a program will be determined by various factors specific to each campus. Things to consider include the organizational structure of computing on campus, lab requirements, available space, available funds, and available staff. Campus administration philosophy and policy will have an influence on where and how services are set up.

Have the task force answer these questions to help determine where the adaptive computing technology support and services should be physically based. What commitment do you have from your school administrators? How does this affect lab placement? Do university executives understand the legal requirements of the Rehabilitation Act of 1973, Sections 503 and 504, and are they familiar with the Americans with Disabilities Act?

Services and equipment available to the general campus population and the existing services for disabled students will play a role in how adaptive computing technology and services are implemented or enhanced and consequently where the services are housed. Before making recommendations, consider these questions: How do your current support programs for students with disabilities operate? Do you have a single computer lab or multiple labs? Who staffs and funds the labs? What adaptive equipment is in the labs? Do individuals, divisions, departments, or schools have their own dedicated labs? Are there completely self-sufficient labs to support students with disabilities, or are such labs dependent on other campus resources? Is there a central controlling office, such as the provost office, a disabled student services office, or a 504-ADA compliance office that directs computer access labs and programs to support students with disabilities?

The size, geography, and available transportation on a campus are also factors to consider. For smaller campuses where all facilities are within easy walking distance, a central lab might be the best location for adaptive computing facilities. In a larger setting where buildings may be spread over a wide geographic area, a network of labs distributed across campus would be a good choice. Examine the answers to these questions: Where are classes located? Where is the library? How long will it take a blind person or a person in a wheelchair to navigate the distance between classrooms and the library, or from class to the adaptive lab? Is weather a factor? Heavy snows or rains might preclude a student from getting to a lab located far from classrooms. Facility access for ramps, doors, aisle widths, parking, elevators, restroom facilities, lighting, water fountains, and transportation are all important factors when selecting the type of adaptive lab location that is best for your campus.

Three Approaches to Distributing Equipment

There are three basic approaches to integrating adaptive computing technology services. One is to centralize services and equipment so that they are all located in one place on campus. The second approach is to distribute services and equipment. The third approach is to have a support system that combines the centralized and distributed approaches. There are advantages and disadvantages to each of the three models, and people at each campus should consider their unique resources and requirements when they determine which approach is best at their school.

Centralized Services

An advantage to setting up a central location specifically for adaptive computing technology services is that it offers individualized support for the special needs of disabled students. A central location also makes it easier to train several students at the same time in the use of specific kinds of adaptive equipment. A centralized lab provides more cost-effective use of special adaptive equipment. For example, if your campus has 10 blind students, each using a different lab, you might need ten screen-reading programs and 10 speech synthesizers. But if you have 10 blind students using the same lab, they will be able to get by with two or three sets of that same technology and less support from service providers. In a centralized lab, staff members can be trained and cross-trained on various types of adaptive computing technology, and generally it requires fewer people who are specially trained on adaptive technology to staff one center than to be stationed in various places across campus.

There are also disadvantages to the centralized approach. First, the lab may not be able to replicate the diversity of computing equipment found in general or discipline-specific computing labs elsewhere on campus. Also, a centralized lab separates students with disabilities from mainstream computer facilities and support, which may mean that the students will have difficulty accessing discipline-specific and instructional software. Additionally, a centralized lab may create an environment in which students miss the personal contact with lab consultants, teachers' assistants, and peers.

Distributed Services

Setting up distributed adaptive computing services through an academic computing office offers several advantages. This approach may be the most equitable, by providing adaptive equipment in various labs located throughout the campus. The academic computing office may be best equipped to provide "reasonable accommodation" for discipline-specific computing and access to instructional software, because specialized computer configurations such as CAD-CAM cannot always be replicated in a lab dedicated to disabled students. Offering distributed services makes use of existing computer lab space, trained staff, and existing computer equipment. This may be an advantage in seeking funding. More than one college campus has acquired additional funding for adapted hardware and software and for training students and existing computer staff in the use of enhanced computer applications.

There are, however, some disadvantages to this system. Some service providers feel that the distributed method offers less support for the specialized training necessary for the use of adaptive computing and for maintaining state-of-the-art adaptive computing information. There may be a lack of administrative coordination, which may result in insufficient continuity of staff support to maintain high-quality services.

Combined Approach

A third option is to combine centralized and distributed services by setting up a main resource lab for students with disabilities while also having adaptive computing technology available at the general computing facilities on the campus. Apart from the services offered in a specialized lab, actual computer access can be widely distributed across campus, its placement depending on need: in public-access labs, in the library, or in specialized discipline-specific facilities. This approach offers a center where students can get individualized support at a specific location at the same time that it allows students to make use of other computer sites on the campus.

The disadvantage to this arrangement is that the distributed computing centers on campus may expect the central coordinating unit to provide all support services, which may keep them from developing their own capacity to serve users with disabilities. This approach may also inhibit the mainstreaming intent of the distributed approach.

STRATEGY THREE: USE THE ADAPTIVE LAB AS A CAMPUS RESOURCE

An adaptive computing lab can be an important campus resource. This lab could be in its own location or within a larger, general-purpose computing facility. Such a lab is an ideal focal point for several activities:

- Demonstrations of technology can be given to disabled students and staff, computing center support staff, campus employees and departments, local businesses, government officials, K–12 special education teachers, vocational rehabilitation personnel, and the media. Demonstrations are a great way to raise people's awareness of the availability and potential use of adaptive technology.
- Access barriers and approaches for individual students and staff with disabilities can be assessed. Don't overlook the possibility of providing assessments for outside groups as a means to generate income for your center.
- Training can be provided for students, faculty, and staff on adaptive computing equipment. Training people outside the center as a fee service may also be an income-producing activity.
- Public access computers with adaptive technology can be made available to students who need special equipment. These would provide access to announcements, job listings, and other types of general information provided campuswide.
- Adaptive computing technology can be evaluated to determine its effectiveness for campus use. This would normally be handled best in a resource lab. Special devices for instructional software (such as CAD-CAM) can be evaluated in a distributed lab.
- Workshops for educators, businesses, and vocational rehabilitation can be hosted as a community service or a fee service.
- Public programs can be offered to raise the level of awareness on your campus and in your community to the educational and employment opportunities for people who are disabled. Solicit the assistance of your campus public relations department and the local media. Invite

the president of your university, the mayor, the governor, the state superintendent of schools, the state commissioner of vocational rehabilitation, and local businesses.

- A loaner pool of laptop computers, adaptive devices, and software can be maintained for loaning to other labs or disabled students.

STRATEGY FOUR: STAFF THE PROGRAM

One of the most important areas to consider when establishing adaptive computing technology services is staffing. Hiring and maintaining an adequately trained staff is as important—or more important—than purchasing equipment. If a program doesn't have the proper staff support, the equipment will just collect dust. Establish permanent staff positions to ensure continuity in providing support services, and invest in staff training.

Cross-train staff members to avoid problems that staff turnover can have on the timely delivery of support services. For example, if the one staff person familiar with Braille production leaves before the end of a school term, the program might be left with a blind student who can't take final exams or complete coursework.

It might be necessary to phase-in your staff. You might start your program with a half-time support position that will develop into a full-time coordinator position. Staff size will be linked to growth in the demand for services and the increasing complexity and diversity of user needs that come with that growth. This increased demand for services can be anticipated in program proposals with a phased implementation of staff support.

You don't have to acquire staff that are expert in both computing and disability. People who provide adaptive computing technology support services come from a wide variety of backgrounds—sometimes unrelated to computers or to disabilities. Motivated people with good interpersonal skills and the willingness to learn the technology make the best support staff. Technology applications can be learned. Sensitivity to different disability-related needs can be learned. It is possible to start with a disability specialist who can then learn the computer technology, or to start with a technical specialist who can learn about disabilities.

Finding Staff

When you look for candidates to fill staff positions, consider recruiting from the following groups:

- Vocational rehabilitation organizations. They may know of individuals looking for employment who have experience working with people with disabilities.

- Computer classes. Students in computer classes on campus, some of whom may be eligible for work-study, can be a good source of competent staff members. You may find computer "whiz kids" who love to tinker and could be an asset in installing devices, debugging new programs, and getting familiar with new products.
- Teacher-training programs. This is an excellent source of people who have good communication and teaching skills, and you might be able to offer internships to these teachers-in-training. While filling staff positions, they can learn the computer skills necessary to balance their other abilities. Teacher trainees in special education programs may be particularly interested in an opportunity to work in an adaptive computing program.
- Occupational or physical therapy programs. Students in these fields may have experience or an interest in adaptive computer technology.
- Disabled students. A disabled student who has mastered adaptive computing technology for his or her own studies, especially a student who qualifies for work-study, may be interested in working in the adaptive technology center.
- Disability organizations. Check with organizations such as the Easter Seal Foundation or the United Cerebral Palsy Foundation for people who would like to be on your staff or do volunteer work.
- Rehabilitation engineering or rehabilitation education programs. These programs may have degreed people who are good candidates for employment.
- Other adaptive computing centers. Many centers employ staff on a part-time basis; you may be able to share those employees.

How Many Staff Members?

One consideration you'll have when you plan your staff size is how to determine the best ratio of support staff to users requiring adaptive computing services. Begin by considering these questions: What is the number of permanently disabled students versus temporarily disabled students? What is the breakdown of students by type and severity of disability? Does your school's adaptive computing program have a centralized or distributed organization? How many labs do you anticipate establishing on your campus? How many permanent staff positions, part-time or work-study workers, and volunteer workers can you employ? How many hours of lab consultation are provided each day, and for how many days each week? How long has the adaptive support program been in operation? If you have an older program, you may have acquired so many students that you need more employees than you did in the beginning.

Answers to these questions will allow you to make a rough estimate of how many people you need to plan for in your operation. While your campus's demographics and funding will dictate the exact number of people you have on staff, at least one person should be on duty during lab operating hours who knows how to use and maintain the equipment. You should also have one full-time person who can train users on the equipment, and one who can match individuals with appropriate technology. As your lab serves greater numbers of people, you can split those functions and then hire help as it becomes necessary. There is always a learning curve at the time of start-up—so the staff can expect some long and interesting hours as they train themselves and begin to train students who will use the services. Setting the proper staff expectations from the beginning is important for morale.

STRATEGY FIVE: EQUIP THE PROGRAM

Adaptive computing product needs can be determined by examining the use for which the equipment is intended. Computing systems on campuses are commonly used for academic pursuits that can be divided into three categories:

- General application activities (such as word processing)
- Discipline-related computing applications (such as computer-aided design)
- Online information services

It is important that all students—whether or not they have a disability—have access to the computer equipment and support services necessary to complete general application activities and discipline-related applications. Current adaptive technology that accommodates people with most types of disabilities is available for both Macintosh and IBM-compatible systems. Most discipline-specific adaptive needs can also be met by using general adaptive solutions. Adaptive computing equipment is also necessary as a compensatory tool for individuals with disabilities. It allows people to perform tasks that are not usually done on the computer. This includes using computers for class note taking, reading assignments, test taking, researching information, and communicating.

Your campus's requirements—direct requests, the scope of computing requirements, and distribution of disability types—will indicate your program's immediate equipment needs. Those immediate needs will, in turn, determine funding priorities. By selecting equipment that satisfies immediate needs, you will establish a strong foundation for the later implementation of widespread adaptive computing solutions. When adapted equipment is purchased for a campus, you should consider usability, cost, training time and intensity, and transparency of the technology.

Usability

Think about how many students can be served by each purchase. Equipment with the broadest applications can serve the greatest number of students. For example, a screen-reading program with a speech synthesizer would normally be used by blind students. The system could, however, also be helpful to students with learning disabilities or students who have limited ability to turn pages. A speech recognition system can serve people with typing limitations and people with learning disabilities. Look for multipurpose accommodations.

Cost

Get the most for your money. As you determine what equipment would suit your population, also consider how specialized the equipment is. Is there something available that would meet the same requirements—and other requirements as well? It may be best to spend a little more on one device or aid if it will serve multiple purposes, rather than having to purchase several individual devices. Do your homework. Is there a less expensive solution that will provide the same advantages? Make cost comparisons. Check volume discounts, warranties, and maintenance agreement costs. Check for trade-ins.

Training Time and Intensity

Some complex equipment requires a great deal of training time and effort. This can be beyond the resources of your staff, and it can be too much of a burden on the student trying to learn how to use the equipment. In some cases, you may be able to find equipment and systems that will provide the same benefits for a student but without requiring as much training time and effort. This is important both for your students and your staff resources.

Transparency

Look for adapted equipment that doesn't interfere with other computer applications and other users who are not disabled. Most accommodations will fall into this category. Only in rare cases will adaptive accommodations render a system unusable by other people.

STRATEGY SIX: FUND THE PROGRAM

There are two main considerations when you plan how to fund your adaptive computing technology program. First you must consider start-up funding for the program. Then you must consider ongoing support.

Start-up Funding

The acquisition of start-up funding is the first step toward establishing an adaptive technology program. Program set-up costs should provide for the following:

- Hiring and training of staff. This is probably the key to the success of your lab and can be even more important than the kind or amount of equipment you have.
- Acquisition of an initial complement of computer equipment, adaptive devices and aids, and required software.
- Acquisition, furnishing, and adaptation of a site. This would include acquiring special equipment such as adjustable desks and tables, chairs, and special lighting (see Chapter 5).
- Outreach and awareness programs aimed at bringing disabled students into the program. Ensure that students with disabilities, feeder schools, and the community all are aware of your resources. Outreach materials should be available in various formats, including Braille, large print, and audiotape. Enlist the support of your campus public relations department on this project.
- A pilot project that demonstrates the viability of your program. It may convince your chancellor or school administrators to fund your adaptive technology program as a line item in the campus budget.

Ongoing Support

Getting permanent financial support for an adaptive technology program is as crucial as obtaining start-up funding. Unfortunately, some colleges have adequately funded their start-up costs, recruited students and staff, bought equipment—and then have run out of funds to support the services that were implemented. Emphasize the importance of:

- Maintaining the continuity of access services. Once the program is initiated, the ability of many students to continue their education will be impaired if the program is discontinued.
- Meeting legal mandates. The school can spend much more defending itself in a discrimination lawsuit than it would in providing necessary accommodation. Campuses should strive to follow current legal guidelines and anticipate future requirements.
- Program growth. Success for the program means growth for the program. A good support program will increasingly attract people who need the services provided.
- The need for new equipment. Newer technology will become available, and new needs will be identified. You must be in a position to acquire state-of-the-art technology.
- The need for ongoing staff training. You will need to continue to train your staff and students. Ongoing funding must be available.

Develop a Funding Prospectus

There are two possible sources of funding for an adaptive computing program—external and internal. External funding can be important in getting a program off the ground, but internal funding must be obtained to secure the long-term provision of services. Before you approach any source for funding, put together a concise and convincing prospectus that will communicate the purpose and implementation of an adaptive computing program. Your funding prospectus should include the components listed below.

Statement of Rationale

Begin by stating the reasons for providing adaptive computer services for students with disabilities. We have developed a three-pronged rationale that provides a good framework for discussing the need for adaptive computing technology support and services.

- It's the right thing to do. Adaptive technology support and services provide compensatory tools that help disabled students enter and finish school—often when they would not otherwise be able to do so. Adaptive technology also provides the same access to computing services that all other students have.
- It makes economic sense. We currently spend $120 billion a year on support for people with disabilities, yet we spend only $3 billion a year on rehabilitation. With education and training, many people with disabilities can get jobs and help support themselves.
- It's the law. The Americans with Disabilities Act (ADA) mandates that individuals with disabilities must be accommodated in all settings, including schools. Refusing to meet the legal mandate may result in costly court battles and judgments.

Statement of Purpose

Tell how computer access is an integral part of the college or university mission. Discuss the barriers to computer use that exist for some disabled students, tell what adaptive computer technology is, and outline how it will benefit students. State the characteristics of the students who will be assisted, and emphasize how the education process will be improved.

Documentation of Need

Detail how the director of disabled student services, the director of academic computing services, the head librarian, faculty, staff, and students have demonstrated that the need exists. This will be easy if you have already developed a consensus in a team that includes these people. Use as much hard data as you can find—surveys, interviews, and examples of course requirements. Cite other colleges and universities with model programs (see Appendix A). Reiterate the legal obligations of your campus.

Objectives and Activities

List the steps necessary to implement your equipment-acquisition and staff-training plans. Describe how students will be accommodated, who will provide the training, what equipment is required, and where the main sites exist for adaptations to be made available.

Budget

Set up several scenarios for providing accommodations for individual students, and attach a budget to each scenario. The initial step in preparing a budget is to estimate start-up and ongoing costs. Be sure to consider the following costs in your budget:

- Total system costs
- Lab furnishings and renovations
- Staff payroll
- Staff development and training
- Expendible supplies and materials

Armed with a thorough funding prospectus, you're ready to approach various funding sources.

External Fundraising

External funds will come in the form of federal, state, and private grants; corporate and community donations; and matching funds from area businesses.

- Grants. Consider groups, individuals, and foundations that have an interest in people who are disabled and/or in higher education. Obvious candidates include the Easter Seal Foundation, the United Way, the Lions' Club, and other national or regional organizations. Check local groups, too.
- Corporate and community donations. Consider developing a business advisory council to offer advice. Council members make good supporters and potential donors to the program.
- State and federal agencies. Make sure you research the hundreds of funding programs that are available. Start by calling the Tech Act office in your state (see Appendix B for the RESNA office, which can refer you to the Tech Act office in your state).
- Matching funds from local businesses. Publicize what you are doing, and let businesses know that you have a need for funding. Businesses

may have matching grant money or may be willing to donate equipment as they upgrade their own.

- In-kind grants and donations. Promote your program. Businesses are
  receptive to worthwhile programs, especially if they can get some
  publicity. Look for surplus paper, diskettes, and other supplies, as well
  as used furniture and computers, to reduce your expenses. Consider
  running an advertisement in the classified section of your local
  newspaper under the "Computers" section, saying that a nonprofit
  school is in need of computing equipment and supplies to provide a
  program for students who are disabled.
- Alumni. Those with disabilities or who have family members with
  disabilities may be especially interested in your program. Work through
  the alumni office for designated gifts.
- Fees for service. Try to establish a relationship with your state division
  of rehabilitation services (DRS) that will generate funds for your
  program.

Internal Fundraising

Internal funds will come in the form of your college or university's reasonable
accommodation fund; core funding for the program; and cofunding, which is
based on two or more departments contributing to the purchase of equipment.

- Reasonable accommodation fund. Some campuses are starting to
  develop funds to provide all types of accommodations for the campus.
  This may be a source of funding for adaptive technology and equipment.
- Core funding. Propose a permanent budget allocation for adaptive
  technology. This provides the best means for responding to immediate student needs and is a rapid-response mechanism for necessary
  equipment purchases. Departmental funding is often available only
  on a year-to-year basis. A permanent equipment allocation can be
  used to leverage departmental resources through cofunding, matching funds, and loaner equipment.
- Cofunding. Cofunding can stretch limited equipment budgets by
  allowing two or more departments or groups within an institution to
  pool their money to buy equipment that they can share. Some candidates to consider for cofunding are disabled student services, academic computing, and the campus library.
- Matching funds. Get an agreement from your school saying that if you
  can raise a certain amount of money, the school will match your
  funds.

- Flexible funding/leveraging strategies. Think about a loaner pool of equipment, discounted equipment that can be loaned or given from the central lab to distributed labs, and seed equipment that would place a small complement of equipment in a distributed lab to get it started and prove the value of the concept.

STRATEGY SEVEN: IDENTIFY ADDITIONAL PROGRAM BENEFITS

Once your program is in place, what are possible extensions that will benefit students, your campus, and the local community? A forward-looking administration will be interested not only in the immediate plans, but also in the future benefits of your program. Highlight these benefits when you present your overall plan. For example, the program can be expanded to include more students, including home-based students, by creating and teaching distance education classes offered through the Internet.

Workshops for educators and businesses can be conducted on issues relating to disabilities and the uses of adaptive technology. This could be done as a community service or for a fee. You might also hold workshops for rehabilitation professionals and educators that offer continuing education credit.

The program might support or initiate academic courses on adaptive technology and lobby for new degree options that include adaptive computing technology. The program might also offer executive education courses that combine legal issues, disability personnel planning, and adaptive computer technology. This might be a fee-service opportunity sponsored in cooperation with the schools of business, management, or continuing education. A good campus program can become a community resource to K–12 educators, rehabilitation professionals, local and state government, and businesses. This can be very good for your school's public relations and image. The program could conduct research and development on disability products and ways to integrate people with disabilities into society. This could be a cooperative effort with schools of engineering, occupational therapy, and education, among others.

STRATEGY EIGHT: CREATE AN IMPLEMENTATION PROPOSAL

Now that you've put together a task force, analyzed your campus and determined student need, identified a program strategy, and made funding plans, how do you put all of this material into a coherent, presentable form? What components should be included in the implementation proposal that you present to the campus administrators? We suggest you include the following elements, which can be customized to the established administrative guidelines of your campus:

- A mission statement. Write a one- or two-sentence description of what you want your program to accomplish.
- The objectives of your program. Develop a concise statement of what you will accomplish with the resources you are requesting.
- Program rationale. Offer the three-pronged EASI rationale: It's the right thing to do, it makes economic sense, and it's the law.
- Demographics report. Present current and projected demographics for students, faculty, and staff to identify the number of people to be served.
- Model programs. Cite programs on other campuses to demonstrate the viability of adaptive services programs and to show what competitive campuses are doing (see Appendix A).
- Legal mandate statement. Outline the laws with which the university must comply in order to avoid grievances and legal action. This can be one of the major motivations for your campus to implement an adaptive technology program.
- Task force recommendations. Report your task force's recommendations on which department or group should control the adaptive technology program, where to establish the program, and how to fund it. This is an important component of your plan.
- Achievement/retention benefits. Include a statement on the anticipated improvement in the academic achievement of students who have access to technology and the ability of the school to improve the retention rate of these students (see the University of Nebraska study, Table 1.1).
- Staffing recommendations. Indicate how many staff positions you will need. Emphasize the need for quality people and proper training, and suggest possible sources for candidates.
- Needs statement. Detail the funding needs for the program. You may spread this over multiple years, with differing amounts for each year, depending on your implementation plan. Be realistic, but not so conservative that you can make no progress toward your goals. It would not be prudent to exhaust the first year's budget in three months and then have to limit services or go back to ask for additional funding.
- Funding source identification. List funding sources to demonstrate that you have thought about this critical area and have some suggestions for funding sources. Most administrators like creative funding proposals.
- Implementation strategies. Explain how you would start the program. Would you begin with a pilot project in a centralized lab, a small distributed lab in a particular school, something in the library, or some combination of these?

- Time schedule. Establish a timeline. Determine how long it would take you to establish a program and when you would be up to full capacity.
- List of functional units. Identify all school functional units that have individuals with disabilities—students, faculty, or staff—who would benefit from the program.
- Progress report. Specify the points at which you will provide updates to the administration on the program's progress. Suggest an interval long enough to allow you to identify progress but short enough to enable you to ask for assistance, if necessary.
- Task force participants list. List the task force participants with their titles and affiliations.
- Statement of benefits. End with a summary of benefits to students, the university, and the community. State why the project is worth the investment. Include the benefits of compliance, including staying out of court.

ADDITIONAL REMINDERS

Adaptive access guidelines should be in place for all lab sites, and in-house experienced staff should be available to provide services and support. Staff expertise can be developed through interaction with computing services and disabled student services personnel, by attending conferences, and by consulting adaptive technology resources. A hub site for coordinating adaptive services and providing training and advanced support will generally be the most efficient use of resources. Staff should be trained in sensitivity and awareness issues, as well as in the technical aspects of adaptive computing.

Consumer input can be invaluable. Consumers are individuals with disabilities, as well as other students, faculty, and staff. People from diverse areas may be interested in contributing to the development of services.

Seek internal funds from areas that address all student needs, programs, and services that deal with disability-related issues, and departments and colleges that have disabled students enrolled in their disciplines. Charitable organizations, disability-related foundations, state agencies, and vendors are possible sources for external funds and equipment donations.

Awareness sessions where people can discuss the importance of computing skills, the communication and information-gathering capabilities of computers, and computer adaptations should be available. Hold on-campus and off-campus sessions. Go into the community and enlist the aid of organizations and agencies that can be of help.

CHAPTER 5

Creating Accessible Workstations and Facilities

Forty years ago, when people dreamed their "what the future will be like" dreams, they imagined cars that would cruise at 400 miles an hour, robots that would perform all kinds of mundane tasks, and computers that would change the very way we live. Well, today's freeway traffic jams keep most cars cruising less than 20 miles an hour, and robots still haven't shown up in very many homes or offices. But the role that computers play at the end of the 20th century has met, and perhaps surpassed, what was once imagined. Today, computers are used in almost every facet of daily life. Computers have turned up in kindergarten classrooms, libraries, and even corner grocery stores. Almost everyone in our society has one kind of computer contact or another. Our school systems, in particular, have incorporated computing hardware and software into most students' daily curriculum.

Computers have now become commonplace for tasks such as word processing, spreadsheets, information retrieval, and reproduction of historic and statistical information. At colleges and universities, computers and software are being used for class instruction, for out-of-class assignments, and to gain access to information. They are being used for campus administration and enrollment. Setting up adaptive computing services for people with disabilities has a twofold purpose. The first is to make campus computing systems and resources accessible to everyone. The second is to provide compensatory computing tools that can help students and staff with disabilities accomplish various tasks more efficiently.

With 10.5 percent of all postsecondary students reporting a disability of some kind, it has become imperative that as a college or university establishes computer services for the general campus population, it must also plan services for disabled students and staff.

WHERE SHOULD ACCESS BE PROVIDED?

All facilities on a college or university campus must be accessible to students with disabilities. Ideally, all campus facilities that provide access to computer services would also offer appropriate adaptive technology to be used as compensatory tools.

Computer Lab Access

Two kinds of computer labs should be considered when you set out to make computing accessible to your disabled students and staff. The first type of computer facility is available to the general campus population. These labs are typically operated by the campus central computing office, and students use the labs to work on class assignments, do research, and access electronic information. Also in this category is the departmental, divisional, or school computer lab that is open only to that section's own students. For example, the law school might have a computer lab open only to law school students. Generally, this type of lab contains software and information that is necessary to the particular students who are allowed to use it.

The second type of computer facility is the special adaptive computing lab, available only to students and staff with disabilities. Generally, these labs are for student assessment, equipment evaluation, training, and student use.

Library Access

Libraries are used by every college and university student. Adaptive computing service providers should be prepared to offer guidance and assistance to the library staff to help them plan and implement physical access to library facilities for disabled users, as well as access to the computer equipment necessary to use the library catalog and other computerized information (see also Chapters 10 and 11).

Dormitory Access

Some schools provide computers in dormitories for student use. These schools should make accommodations for disabled students who live in the dorms. Service providers should be prepared to offer suggestions to help plan dormitory computer access.

Student Center Access

Many schools have computers at strategic locations around campus. These computers, which may provide access to campuswide information systems, must be able to accommodate disabled students.

Bookstore Access

The campus bookstore is one of the most widely used facilities on campus. Some have computers to look up stock location and price information. These computers must be accessible by students and staff who are disabled.

ACCESS GUIDELINES

Whether you are setting up a new lab, reconfiguring an existing lab, or looking over your facility to see if it is accessible to all users, there are certain basic physical access issues to examine.

Space Considerations

The first thing to consider when setting up a computer facility that will accommodate people with disabilities is physical access to the lab. Before the academic computing world knew about the many new technologies that can assist computer users with disabilities, wheelchair access was the only environmental accommodation made in computing labs. Now, when a workstation in the university computing environment might have a Braille printer, voice recognition, special keyboards, input devices, and other peripherals, it is easy to overlook some of the basic physical barriers that might hinder or block a disabled person's access into and around a computing site.

Direct and accessible wheelchair routes must be provided to all buildings and rooms that house computer workstations to be used by students or staff with disabilities. Don't forget to make arrangements for nearby accessible restrooms and telephones. When electric doors can be provided, they should have electric eye or remote-control activation. Signs pointing out accessible entrances, elevators, and restrooms should be prominently displayed.

The floor plan of a computer lab can mean the difference between accessibility and inaccessibility for students and staff members who use wheelchairs. The room or area should allow enough floor space for an individual to easily maneuver his or her wheelchair to and from the adaptive workstations. Sixty inches is the minimum required width for an aisle that will allow a person to pivot his or her wheelchair and pull up to a desk. Seventy inches or more is required for a wheelchair or scooter to turn around. It may be necessary to remove one or two workstations from a lab in order to provide full wheelchair access. If an access accommodation has been made for a particular individual, keep the feature in place for eventual use by other individuals.

Whether adapted computer devices are going to be integrated into the general campus computing facility or located in a special lab designed specifically for the use of students with disabilities, it is also important to provide enough space for training. If possible, space should be partitioned from the general work area so that training and demonstrations can take place without disturbing other computer users. In many cases, however, training equipment will serve double duty as lab access equipment, so this will not be possible.

Workstation Location

If possible, the computer workstations accessible to disabled staff and students should not be located in a separate room within the lab facility. It is important for the user with a disability to have ready access to lab consultants, teaching assistants, special software, and fellow students who might be forming study groups.

Generally speaking, it is a good plan to situate adapted workstations close to the main lab entrance and on the outer end of a bank or row of workstations. This keeps people who use wheelchairs, scooters, crutches, or service dogs from having to navigate through crowded aisles. Also, take care to ensure that the area has no protruding objects or other hard-to-see hazards that would be dangerous to a blind person or a person with limited vision.

General Workstation Accommodations

Adjustable-height tables can allow computer access for people with various disabilities. It is important that the adjustment controls are in locations accessible to people with limited mobility or reach and that they are easy to use by those with limited strength. If you cannot afford adjustable tables, a limited solution that will help wheelchair users is to place two-inch-thick blocks of wood under the table legs. However, this may be inconvenient for other users, because it generally makes the table too high for comfortable use.

Adjustable tables or stands that tilt the monitor can be used to reduce glare and enhance the user's view of the screen. Adjustable height and tilt of the keyboard is also a necessity for some people, especially those in wheelchairs, people who wear braces, and individuals who are very short. A tilted keyboard is also helpful for those with limited hand and wrist motion and for people using mouthsticks. For a person with no arms or limited upper extremity mobility, it might even be necessary to place the keyboard on the floor.

Seating and position provisions may be necessary for a person with spinal cord injury. A special adjustable chair or a stand-up board may be required. A person using a stand-up board may also need adjustments to the keyboard position and table height. Always consult with a specialist when making position recommendations for a person who has any type of mobility impairment. This will help ensure that positioning strategies do not inadvertently cause physical injury to the person.

Power strips can be used to switch on and off an entire system when normal power switches are difficult to reach. External disk drives and power switches with extended cables also offer flexibility in positioning, which allows better access for people with mobility impairments. Extra lighting may be required for people with some types of vision impairment or learning disabilities, and soft lighting and glare screens are helpful for those with low vision or certain learning disabilities.

Since workstations for students with disabilities generally have special equipment, a policy statement or appropriate sign should be posted stating that nondisabled students will be expected to move to other workstations when a disabled person needs access to the adapted workstation. Generally it's a good idea to have a sign-up sheet for adapted equipment, but the lab should also make accommodations for a student with an emergency. Common courtesy will normally prevail, but posted regulations establish the computer lab's policy and will reduce misunderstandings and other problems.

Most of these accommodations are common sense once you have had the chance to assess the capabilities of an individual student or staff member. The important thing is to make the lab accessible in the most beneficial and least costly way. Some of the most successful adaptive labs and workstations are run by creative people who look at each requirement as a challenge that they'll meet by doing "whatever works."

Access for People with Severe Disabilities

A person with a severe disability may require several adaptive devices and aids. This gets tricky if the solutions come from different vendors, and it may take some trial and error to determine whether all the combinations of technology can coexist with the hardware and software being used. It is worth investigating to determine if there is one vendor who can provide the whole solution for an individual with complex needs. If not, one vendor who can provide most of the solution may be able to suggest a source to provide the other necessary equipment or software. If the vendors involved have representatives in your area, it would be a good idea to ask them to come to your site and assist in the evaluation and trial of their products. Any agreement to purchase equipment should be contingent upon the success of a total solution for your user.

The involvement of the disabled individual in selecting assistive devices and technology is essential, especially since he or she may be able to suggest solutions based on prior use of a computing package in another school, at home, or in the job environment. Avoid new adaptive solutions that are complex and may be too difficult for some disabled individuals to learn or use. Many adaptive computing solutions will require extra training on the part of the lab consultant and the person using the equipment.

Once a workstation is configured and operational for a severely disabled student, you should try to provide total campus information access from that terminal. Due to cost considerations, other computer sites on campus might not be able to duplicate the configuration at first, so it will be best to set up the workstation so that when the disabled student or staff member is in the lab, he or she can access any other information that may be needed, including shared campus information resources, electronic library catalogs, and online course information.

BASIC EQUIPMENT CONFIGURATIONS

Since staff and students with disabilities must have access to the same resources as their nondisabled peers, adaptive workstations should be configured according to standard system requirements used at the college or university. Completely customizing adaptive workstations can become an obstacle to providing integrated access. Besides adapted labs or workstations, disabled students must also have access to software and peripheral devices that enable computer access.

Basic configurations should be developed for accommodating major disability categories. The basic configurations can then be modified for individual needs. The basic disability categories are vision impairments, mobility impairments, hearing impairments, learning disabilities, speech impairments, and traumatic brain injuries.

The following basic configurations were adapted from workstations being used by the University of Missouri. Use them as a guide to create your own workstations. These configurations have a combination of adapted accommodations for people who are blind (B), have low vision (LV), are mobility impaired (MI), are learning disabled (LD), or are hearing impaired (H). See also Chapter 8.

Adaptive Workstation No. 1

Electric, adjustable table
IBM PS/2 Model 70 (B) (LV)
IBM PC or compatible with 12 mb of RAM
AccentSA external voice synthesizer
Vista 2 (LV)
Vantage CCTV (LV)
Kensington Expert Mouse trackball (MI)
Superkey (MI)
ChiWriter (MI)
Grammatik IV (LD)

Some of these accommodations may also be useful for people with learning disabilities or traumatic brain injuries, as well as for the listed disability groups. For instance, a person with a learning disability may be able to "read" electronic documents by listening to the text using a screen-reading program with a speech synthesizer. Similarly, people with certain types of learning disabilities have success when they can enlarge the size of characters on a screen using devices such as Vista and Vantage or by changing the color combination of characters on a screen. The screen magnification program Zoom Text by AI Squared gives the option of redefining colors as it magnifies. The configuration shown for Workstation No. 1 gives a good cross section of devices and technology useful for the major disability groups.

Adaptive Workstation No. 2

Artic Business Vision (B) (LV)
Romeo Braille printer (B)
Duxbury translator (B) (converts text to Grade II Braille)
Inmac sound cover (to minimize the Braille printer sound)
Kensington Expert Mouse trackball (MI)
Superkey (MI)
Grammatik IV (LD)
IBM AccessDOS (MI) (H)

As noted for Workstation No. 1, some of the devices listed for Workstation No. 2 may have use for people with learning disabilities or traumatic brain injuries, as well as for the disability categories listed. Artic Business Vision could be useful to a learning disabled person by allowing him or her to "read" text aurally from a screen. A voice recognition program like IBM VoiceType or DragonDictate would be beneficial to a person with a mobility impairment and possibly to a person with a learning disability or a traumatic brain injury.

Adaptive Workstation No. 3

Macintosh Power Mac
outSPOKEN (B) (LV) (LD)
Headmaster (head pointing device for people who cannot use a keyboard and mouse) (MI)
Vantage CCTV (LV)
Kensington Expert Mouse trackball (MI)
Power Secretary (MI)
Grammatik Mac (LD)
Easy Access (MI)
ScreenDoors, an on-screen keyboard with prediction (MI)
Co:Writer (LD)
Telepathic (LD)

As with the IBM configurations, Macintosh outSPOKEN allows a person with a vision impairment or learning disability to listen to text on the screen. Close View, which comes with every Macintosh, provides large-print screen characters for people with low vision. Vantage is a closed-circuit television that displays hard copy in large characters. Easy Access also comes as standard equipment with every Macintosh. It allows two key commands to be entered consecutively, instead of simultaneously. This feature is useful for people typing with one finger or with a mouthstick or a headwand. The trackball is easier for some people to maneuver than a mouse. Grammatik, a grammar checker, coupled with a spelling checker, can be valuable to people with learning disabilities. The Power Secretary enables a person with a mobility impairment to issue Macintosh commands by voice.

A keyguard can be used on any of the three configurations to accommodate a person who has a hand tremor or difficulty in striking a single key. The keyguard is a piece of plastic with a hole positioned over each key. A person can use one finger, a hand-brace pointer, or a mouthstick to depress the desired key without striking adjacent keys.

Each of these basic workstation configurations is designed to meet basic requirements for accommodating the major disability categories listed earlier. You'll probably need to customize workstations for certain individuals or for your particular campus, but these workstations are a good starting place.

DOCUMENTATION

It is critical to document the basic configurations of workstations and of the entire lab. When people set up adaptive computer labs or workstations, they often overlook the importance of developing the proper hardware and software documentation for disabled users and making it available in appropriate formats, including Braille, audiotape, large print, and on disk. Documentation should include step-by-step instructions for performing various tasks and for identifying the locations of adaptive packages and workstations.

Ideally, all documentation for standard and adaptive equipment should be provided in an ASCII format on both Macintosh and IBM-compatible floppy disks. This will allow easy conversion into other, more accessible formats. For example, information from an ASCII file can be displayed in a magnified form on the computer screen or printed in enlarged text for persons with vision impairments. For people who are blind, an ASCII text format can either be spoken from the computer screen using voice output or printed in Braille. Voice output is also helpful for some individuals who cannot turn the pages of a book.

For documentation not provided in ASCII format, several approaches are available for providing access. A scanner with optical character recognition can be used to scan text into a computer and convert the material to alternative formats. Devices other than computers, such as closed-circuit televisions, are also available to enlarge text in books or brochures.

Additionally, each adaptive device at a workstation should be labeled with an identification of its function. These signs should also be produced in large print and Braille for people with vision impairment. In addition to helping users who are disabled, labels will assist the lab consultants, who may need to be knowledgeable about many devices. Descriptive labels will also increase the awareness of all people who use the computer lab of the campus's commitment to support all students and staff who have disabilities.

CHOOSING TECHNOLOGY AND EQUIPMENT

Campus Demographics

Determine the number of people with disabilities who need or want to use the campus computing facilities. Answer these questions: What are your students' and staff's disabilities? What is the severity of their disabilities? What are their reasons for using computers? Use the answers to divide the disabled population on your campus into major disability categories.

Identify the existing computer-access barriers for disabled individuals in each category. When reviewing access barriers, consider these questions: Is you campus hilly? Is it sprawling, with classes located far from general computer labs? Is it multilevel and hard to navigate for vision-impaired or mobility-impaired individuals? How many people use wheelchairs? How many people will need complex adaptations, and how many need something simpler, such as a raised table? Based on general computer usage at your school, what role can adaptive technology play in providing access for the individuals on campus? Are there any alternatives to adaptive technology?

Consider input from students with disabilities. Designing a solution without the contributions of the people involved is like asking a person who has never driven a car to design a car for others to drive. Disabled students and staff may have previous experience that will be valuable in planning your campus's immediate acquisitions.

Long-Range Projections

As plans are made for today's adaptive computing workstations, make sure that you consider probable future trends. Although you can't look into a crystal ball to see what specific students in the future will need, you can estimate their requirements by considering demographic trends of the K–12 feeder schools in your area. Also remember to consider the estimated changes in college and university disability demographics that will probably occur because of new computer access and support services. Be sure to include plans for the major campus mainframe operating system, cabling, and campus network changes. Consider what technology is likely to fit your requirements in the future and what funding will be available for support. You should think about technical and nontechnical considerations when you choose adaptive equipment.

Technical Considerations

Think about the general use for which each piece of equipment or technology is intended. Do you need more than one copy of certain software programs? If you're buying software, what license restrictions apply? Can you use a software program on more than one system or over a network?

Consider hardware compatibility. Is the adaptation that you're considering usable on IBM, IBM compatibles, and on Macintosh? Do you need a different version of software for each platform on your campus?

Try to develop transparent solutions so that your adapted workstations are usable by all students and staff. Is the adaptation transparent to *all* the programs it will need to work with and support? Has it been tested with your word processors, spreadsheets, utility programs, and campuswide information systems? Will it work with your emulators when attached to a host system? Will it work with Microsoft Windows?

Work to develop the most flexible system possible. Can a particular adaptation work with other adaptations that are on the same system? How difficult is it to remove and reinstall the adaptation? Consider that some adaptations may be software and BIOS-level sensitive and will contend for the same interrupt level from a keyboard. Work to establish ease of connection to other systems. How easy is it to connect a device to the main system? Does the device also require software to operate?

Control the memory requirements of any system you propose. How much memory is required to operate a terminate-and-stay-resident (TSR) program? Is there sufficient memory on your target system?

Consider maintenance costs, as well as purchase costs. How are program fixes or hardware engineering changes distributed, and at what cost? What technical support is available from the vendor, and during what hours and at what additional cost? Examine warranty contracts. Are there warranty options? What are they, and at what cost?

Make sure that all your adaptive solutions are compatible with DOS, Macintosh, UNIX, OS/2, emulation, RISC/6000, or other operating systems used on your campus. Most IBM and IBM-compatible solutions will operate only with IBM/MS-DOS. Other operating systems may or may not work with an emulator. Check this before you make a purchase.

Other Considerations

In addition to those technical considerations, think about the following criteria in the product selection process.

Examine disability-related barriers. An individual's stamina, attention span, need for attendant care, finger and manual dexterity, overall coordination, and sensitivity to fumes, odors, or dust, may affect his or her ability to use a computer workstation.

Be creative as you meet the needs of individuals. Physical abilities, computing aptitude, and previous experience of the individual is important, and you might be able to devise special solutions to meet special needs. For example, if a student comes to the campus from a nearby high school where he or she used highly specialized adaptive equipment, it might be possible to borrow or purchase those accommodations from the school. This might be an acceptable solution to meeting one individual's needs, as long as the college or university is not responsible for loss or damage to the equipment and it is compatible with the campus's operating environment. Try to find out if there are other colleges and universities in your system that are involved in an exchange pool that arranges to lend or trade adaptations not currently being used. If there isn't, considering establishing one.

Consider current and future task requirements as you make equipment purchases. What tasks are required of your students right now? Again, look to your campus demographics and determine the grade level of your population, as well as disability type. If you have a freshman bulge in the population, you may have a lot of students who need software that will help them in composition classes now, but down the line you may have a greater number of students looking for software to support law classes. Try to acquire equipment and software that will meet today's needs and also will be useable for future requirements.

Look at existing adaptive technology. What's already in your lab? What's in the marketplace today? How effective is it?

Perhaps most important, consider the training resources of your lab. No technology—hardware or software—is worth anything if you can't hire the staff to train people in how to use it. How will lab consultants be trained on the accommodations? What support will a vendor provide? How much time can be allocated for the lab consultant to train the person who will be using the accommodation?

AVOIDING OBSOLESCENCE

A last, important consideration when purchasing adaptive devices is anticipated obsolescence of the equipment. Explore as much of the existing equipment in the marketplace as you possibly can, regardless of price. This will give you a broad knowledge of solutions for accommodating computer access. This knowledge base can be used when making compatibility and cost decisions as well.

As you purchase equipment, be sure to keep in mind the ongoing technical support that must be provided to avoid technological obsolescence of adaptive computing equipment. This support includes maintenance and upgrading of adaptive devices, troubleshooting compatibility problems with existing and new computer systems, and accommodating new demands that will be placed on the system.

Research new equipment, and acquire as much product information as you can before making a purchase. Do adaptive technology vendors announce future products? Do they have programs to beta-test their products, and would they agree to a joint project with your school? Try to negotiate with vendors before making a purchase. In particular, look at a vendor's upgrade and trade-in policies. Have your agreements written into your purchase contract, or write a letter of understanding about what you expect. You may be dealing with an agent of a vendor, and you really need to have a commitment from the vendor itself.

Understand the need to support graphics. Are the word processing programs, spreadsheets, desktop publishing, and other programs your students will use graphics based, or are they ASCII text based?

Remember to anticipate new demands that will occur in your program. Think about what you expect to be using in one, two, or three years. You may have a budget that won't allow much choice in buying equipment, but at least understand the ramifications of your purchasing reasoning. While new adaptations will become available at an increasingly fast pace, the accommodations you acquire will most likely remain in place for a long time. They may not be the latest model on the market, but if they fulfill your institution's needs, they're worth keeping.

PRACTICAL CONSIDERATIONS FOR LAB LIFE

There are also practical considerations involved in setting up and maintaining adapted computer workstations. Problems sometimes arise because ordinary, mundane things are overlooked.

Air Conditioning

Both electrical equipment and people will raise the temperature in a room. Balance that with the knowledge that some individuals with orthopedic disabilities may have problems maintaining body temperature, so they need a warmer environment. Keep a reasonable temperature, and advise those for whom it is too cool to wear a sweater or a wrap.

Static Electricity

Make sure carpets don't cause electrical problems that could injure students or damage equipment. You might want to place rubber mats at adapted workstations to protect individuals in battery-operated wheelchairs.

Electrical Outlets

Safe electrical outlets and proper grounding are mandatory. A student who uses a speech synthesizer, a closed-circuit television, or other electrical devices will require numerous outlets. Switches must be easily accessible for people with arm or hand limitations. It's important to have enough outlets strategically placed to support equipment, but they shouldn't become a safety hazard for people who use wheelchairs or for those who are blind.

Noise Level

Workstations that use voice synthesis should be placed so that they don't disturb other users. Partitions help reduce the noise level, as does a floor covering. (Rubber floor coverings reduce sound at the same time that they decrease static electricity.) Headsets should be available for people using voice synthesis. Sound covers should be purchased for all Braille printers, but they won't adequately filter all the noise, so you should also try to place the equipment where it won't bother other computer lab users.

Overhead Lighting Glare

While glare is annoying for any computer user, it can make things especially difficult for a person with vision impairment or a learning disability. Sometimes soft lamps or antiglare screens relieve this problem.

Restroom and Telephone Access

Restroom facilities and phones should be in close proximity to the adapted workstation or lab, and they must be clearly marked with signs in appropriate formats.

Medical Emergency and Evacuation Plans

There should be a detailed plan for the actions that lab personnel should take in various emergencies. If possible, one person on each lab consulting shift should be trained in CPR and emergency medical procedures. Keep a list of phone numbers to call for various medical emergencies. While privacy is important, it is a good idea to know if a student has emergency medication such as insulin or nitroglycerin.

Equipment Security

Plan a security system that will ensure that adaptations are not removed from the lab without authorization. Also, you must ensure that licensed programs are on a fixed disk and that they are not copied from a local area network in violation of your license agreement.

SUMMARY OF OVERALL GUIDELINES

To begin, look at the easiest, least expensive approaches to providing computing access and compensatory technology for the students and staff on your campus who have disabilities. Move to more expensive, more complicated approaches only when the simpler ones won't work. Don't hesitate to use high-tech solutions when they're necessary, just don't jump to them unnecessarily. Try simple solutions. Sometimes just tilting a monitor will eliminate the glare that makes it impossible for a person with low vision to read information on a screen.

Ask about your students' prior experiences when you make an evaluation of campus needs. Some students have been using adaptive technology and computers for several years, and they have discovered what they need. Be careful here, though. Some students "know" that they need a particular program or piece of equipment and insist on having that and nothing else. Often they haven't tried other hardware or software that may be a better solution for them. So, although you should solicit students' input, try to keep them from getting stuck using certain solutions just because they always have.

Anticipate progressive disabling conditions. If a person has retinitis pigmentosa, a hereditary degeneration of the retina that will ultimately result in blindness, and the condition is progressing rapidly, it may be advisable to suggest a screen-reading program with a speech synthesizer, rather than recommending a screen-magnification solution. Enabling the person to train on the screen reader while there is still some residual vision will help him or her understand screen spatial relations with the screen reader.

Use adaptive systems that don't interfere with the normal use of a system. Make sure that alternative keyboards can be used with standard keyboards. Connections and software are available that allow both to be operational at the same time. You do not want to have to connect and disconnect keyboards every time an individual with a disability uses the lab. Ideally, solutions should not interfere with a nondisabled person's use of a computer.

Solicit experience and information from others, including occupational, physical, and speech therapists; vendors; disability organizations; other schools; libraries and businesses; and Tech Act offices.

CHAPTER 6

Scope and Limits of Supporting Students with Disabilities

A director of an adaptive computing facility at a large community college tells of a student who demanded that one of the staff give him an injection of medicine every day when he came to the lab. The student was sure that the technician was able to give the injection properly and equally sure that the Americans with Disabilities Act mandated that someone in the lab was responsible for providing that level of medical support. The director was eventually able to convince the student to get his daily injection elsewhere, and the situation didn't get to court. But it's pretty certain that had the student sued the college for such support, the student would have lost. There's no reason that a person trained to work with computers should administer medication to a student with a disability.

This story was relatively clear cut, but sometimes it's not so obvious what types of support services a school should offer. Although service providers should be ready to help disabled students and staff as much as possible, there are limits—both legal and practical—to what services and assistance can be provided. Should a student who needs material in Braille be required to learn how to use the equipment and to produce the needed documents, or is it mandatory that school staff produce them? Should adaptive lab staff be responsible for proctoring tests, or should the professor or a teaching assistant come to the lab to administer exams taken by computer? How much personal assistance should a lab staff member offer—or be required to provide—to a disabled student or staff member?

This chapter considers the scope of services that are necessary to help students and staff with disabilities use the computing services available on a campus. Regardless of the type of service delivery organization your campus chooses to establish, there are several things that are important for the people providing the adaptive computing services to keep in mind. Among these are individual needs assessments, training strategies, consulting responsibilities, media conversion, and the provision of materials in alternative formats.

NEEDS ASSESSMENTS

Providing services for an individual with a disability begins with an individual needs assessment that considers factors unique to that person. It is beyond the scope of this book to detail the complete medical and physiological needs-assessment process, but some of the important components are itemized below.

Identify the person's disability. Is the person blind or vision impaired? Is the person hard of hearing or deaf? If the person has a mobility impairment, what is its extent? Usually there will be a combination of factors that should be taken into account. You may want to do some trial-and-error testing to survey the limits of the person's abilities. Be sure to find out if the person's condition is stable, deteriorating, or improving. For example, if you have a student with low vision whose vision is deteriorating, you might want to provide a speech synthesizer and screen-reading package, rather than using enlarged text strategies. Helping the student become familiar with the speech synthesizer while he or she still has some eyesight will make it easier to use the technology later, when he or she has lost all vision.

Identify how the person's particular disability makes computer use difficult. For example, blind people will not be able to see the computer screen. People with mobility impairments may have trouble using a keyboard. Be sure to ask about the person's prior experience using a computer. If the person does have previous computer experience, find out what devices and equipment were used and what strategies were most successful.

Try to determine the person's motivation and commitment to using adaptive computer technology, and find out if the person is willing to invest the time needed to learn to use the adaptive devices. Some students prefer to have someone else do required typing or reading and aren't really motivated to learn new technology to perform these tasks. It sometimes takes persuasion to get people to take responsibility for their own lives, but it does help prepare them for the world of employment where they will be expected to do a complete job.

Find out what the individual ultimately wants to accomplish. Are the goals reasonable? Don't discourage people who have identified goals in which the obstacles are insurmountable. Instead, encourage them to be realistic about their options and their choices.

Consider, step by step, each individual task a person must accomplish to achieve specific goals. Look at what work is required in an academic setting—reading, writing, processing information, speaking, and listening. After this analysis, you can determine what technology and support might meet a student's needs. Identify the computer systems the person will need access to in order to meet particular goals. An individual may need a computer with word processing, spreadsheet, database, instructional, or other software. The person may need access to the library online system and CD-ROMs or may need to use the campus mainframe for statistics or programming. Find out if the person needs access to local or national network services.

Remember that not all goals are long term, and that you must be sure to consider short-term goals as well. For short-term goals, identify specifically what the person wants to do—read textbooks for a class, write a term paper, communicate orally, or organize information? Choose the best strategy for the short-term goal.

Before you recommend particular equipment for a person, consider also that individual's working environment. Find out where that person spends the most time—in the classroom, at home, in the computer lab, in an individual workstation—and what equipment or devices he or she is already using.

Keep things as simple as you can. After you've considered an individual's personality, needs, and goals, begin your prescription process at the simplest level and work up from there. Sometimes the best fixes are the easiest fixes.

Try not to reinvent the wheel. Adaptive computers have been used in campus labs for a number of years, so you're not sailing in uncharted waters. In most cases, somebody has already experienced the same or a similar situation to the one you are encountering. Consult as many people as you can, and use their expertise.

Remember that the training time and difficulty level must also meet the needs of your student. If the system you recommend is difficult and takes too much training time and effort, your student may get frustrated and give up. Although a less demanding system may not have as many benefits, if the training is more in tune with the student's skills and patience level, it might be a better bet.

Keep in mind the long-range goals and growth of the student as you design a package to meet immediate needs. Try to recommend programs that will be adaptable and practical as the student progresses and makes transitions into other environments, such as employment. Try to choose adaptive equipment that will provide access for more than one area of disability. For example, a screen reader can be used by anyone with a vision impairment or a perceptual disability of the type found in some learning disabilities or by anyone who tires easily while reading the screen.

Provide ongoing assessment and evaluation for every student. Once you determine a system of software and hardware for a person, the inclination is to think that the job is done. But it's important to periodically reassess and reevaluate each student's goals and progress. Needs may change, and technology is always evolving. Don't let students get stuck using old systems when something may have come along to meet their needs better. At the same time, if a system is working well, don't change it just because there is new technology available. The goal is to help the student be productive—not to use new technology simply because it is on the market.

Don't hesitate to refer students to people with more expertise in particular areas. While there are many instances in which you can make recommendations on equipment and systems for students, it is often necessary to refer students to outside professionals. Most service providers will refer a student with a communication disorder to a specially trained speech/communication professional for help with all types of speech systems. Students using Morse code systems that involve sip-and-puff input should also be taught breathing techniques by trained experts. Outside expertise is also recommended for advice on positioning students who use wheelchairs or who have other physical disabilities. Likely sources for local referrals include occupational therapists, rehabilitation centers or hospitals, local branches of the Department of Vocational Rehabilitation, and other adaptive technology resource centers.

Service personnel are the bridge between the technology needed to assist a person with a disability and the academic or job requirements that person is trying to meet. Sometimes it will take creativity and ingenuity to identify the appropriate technology to achieve specific goals. Sometimes it may even be necessary to conclude that some tasks and goals are not achievable by certain individuals, but this conclusion should be reached only as a last resort. The service provider must be an advocate for the person with the disability.

The Southern Connecticut State University has developed the Adaptive Technology Laboratory Start-Up Kit. Its first chapter has intake forms that gather personal information, billing information, education information, employment information, functional information, communication and adaptive device information, health and medication information, other evaluations, computer usage goals, typing experience, and computer experience. This kit is available from:

Southern Connecticut State University
Adaptive Technology Lab, Buley 22
501 Crescent St.
New Haven, CT 06515
Phone: 203-397-4791

TRAINING STRATEGIES

Training people with disabilities to use adaptive equipment is an important function of a service-delivery staff. After you prescribe the equipment and technology to best enhance the student's abilities, you will be in the position of making sure the student is adequately trained to use it.

Generally, training will occur either on a one-on-one basis or as part of a course. The main benefit of individual training is that it is flexible and allows students to progress at their own pace. Some motivated learners can become familiar with a system very quickly, while slower students can move at their own pace. Students in a one-on-one situation also get the undivided attention of the trainer and may feel more comfortable working by themselves than those trained in a classroom situation. To make individual training sessions most effective, it is important to set up a schedule. The schedule will help students know what to expect, both in terms of accomplishments and time. Setting up a schedule with predetermined goals also encourages the student to take the training sessions seriously.

The benefit of training in a group setting is that it provides a structure for students learning adaptive technology. Courses usually begin with the instructor making individual evaluations and designing specific programs for each student. Since one instructor can work with several students at the same time, courses make good use of personnel. The classroom setting also gives students ample opportunity to practice using computers with an instructor nearby to answer questions and give help when it is needed.

The instructional and informational materials on adaptive computing that you compile and use to train your students with disabilities are an important component of your services. Establish a curriculum guide for training students on computer systems. Also, take the time to prepare quick reference guides for frequently used systems, document computer configurations, and note each system's or computer's particular quirks or glitches (this is extremely important).

CONSULTING RESPONSIBILITIES

Service providers often advise other people and departments on campus about adaptive technology options and use. Those in need of consultation include people in the disabled student services office, in the academic computing organization, and in various departments that have students or employees with disabilities; computing support personnel in individual campus departments; and computing facilities people in the campus employment office. The consultation offered by service providers falls into three basic categories— technical, academic, and employment.

Technical advice might include suggesting systems or technology and advising people on how to set up adaptive equipment. Be prepared to train students and staff on adaptive equipment, as well as to perform services such as producing Braille versions of instructional materials. Some students and campus employees will seek your advice on choosing appropriate home computers for class assignments and work.

Academic advice might include making recommendations on access to instructional software and compensatory methods to be used in coursework (be sure to work with the disabled student services office). You'll probably also be asked to help provide access to online information systems and services, including a library online catalog, course schedule, administrative resources, and network services.

Employment advice would include consulting with campus departments about making accommodations for employee workplace computers and about employee access to computers as compensatory tools for work-related tasks such as reading and writing reports, documents, and forms.

MEDIA CONVERSION

Another possible service delivery function is making materials available in formats that will be accessible to everyone. Service-delivery staff might be asked to make both printed and online materials accessible to disabled students and faculty by converting print to computer-readable files and then converting computer-readable files to Braille, large print, and various electronic formats.

When you provide media conversion services for individuals, clearly define the situations in which the service-delivery staff should do the conversion and those in which the person needing the material should do the conversion. For example, if an individual with a disability needs materials converted to large print once or twice a year, the service-delivery staff may want to do the conversion. However, if an individual needs materials converted to Braille on a more frequent basis, it might be appropriate for the individual to learn to convert files. Not only does this save staff time and resources, it's also a valuable skill to learn for future independence in education and employment. Keep in mind that blind students may have difficulty converting scanned materials to Braille because of the necessity for proofreading. It is ultimately the school's responsibility to provide materials in accessible formats, which can include Braille.

The biggest thing to remember about media conversion is that it is time consuming. Before undertaking a conversion project, check with Recording for the Blind and Dyslexic and the National Library Service to see if the material already exists in alternative formats (see Chapter 11). Also make sure that the conversion is warranted and will be useful to a student before committing your staff to media conversion tasks. One service-delivery provider was asked to convert 300 pages of material to Braille for the next week.

When she asked if the student really needed all 300 pages, she was told by the requester that he didn't know exactly what the student needed and thought it would be best to have everything available. When you do a media conversion, keep the computerized version on file in case you have other requests for the same material.

TEST-TAKING ALTERNATIVES

One of the many benefits that computers can offer students with disabilities is an alternative method of taking tests. Blind students and students who can't use their hands to write answers on paper traditionally have had to rely on someone—often their professors—to read them the exam questions, which would then be answered by the student orally. An adapted computer allows more freedom.

Computerized test-taking offers options such as the student using a laptop computer for in-class tests or going to a computer lab to use the equipment there. In either case, certain questions arise. Who is responsible for proctoring the test? What type of software is it permissible for the student to use? How long should the student have to take the test? As a service provider, you should establish certain test-taking procedures. Be prepared to explain to instructors the necessity for computerized test-taking. For example, you may have a student with a learning disability who routinely uses a computerized spelling checker when writing. Yet the student's professor may see the use of that tool during a test as an advantage that amounts to cheating. As the service provider, you'll have to work with instructors to come to a resolution in such situations.

If you establish procedures ahead of time and distribute copies to all of the faculty on your campus, you'll generally have fewer problems with individual cases.

COMPUTER USER GROUPS

As a service provider, you might want to take the time to establish a computer user group on your campus. Such a group can provide an efficient way for individuals who are interested in adaptive technology to learn about access options and to meet with other people who have common interests. A typical user group might meet 6 or 12 times a year. Service providers and adaptive technology manufacturers can be invited to give presentations. A coordinator can work with disabled student services to locate people who might be interested in joining the group.

SUMMARY: THERE'S NOT JUST ONE RIGHT WAY

The most important thing to remember when you're setting up or providing services is that there is no one right way to do it. Some technologies, systems, and methodologies that work well on one campus might be totally unsuitable at another. There are certain services that might be an integral part of service delivery at one school that aren't practical or necessary at another school because of demographics and other considerations. As in every aspect of delivering adaptive computing technology and services, the key is to be flexible and to meet the needs of your campus in the most effective manner available given your campus administration and resources.

CHAPTER 7

Technology and Techniques

Since the day hundreds of thousands of years ago when a person first picked up a stick to grub for roots, humans have been tool users. Through the centuries, our tools have become more and more sophisticated. Today, most of us are routinely using some of the most advanced tools the world has ever known. Obviously, if people who don't have disabilities can use computers to enhance their productivity, then so can people with disabilities. However, disabled people contend with several types of barriers to computer use. Additionally, people with disabilities may have problems accomplishing certain tasks (such as reading, writing, and organizing information), and there are various types of compensatory computing strategies that can help them accomplish those tasks.

This chapter talks about the types of technology available and various techniques that can be helpful to people with disabilities. The information offered here will be relevant both in educational institutions and in the workplace. It is important to understand the difference between *computer access issues* and *compensatory computing strategies,* so you might want to review Chapter 1 to refresh your memory on these two categories within adaptive computing.

The access barriers that limit the ordinary use of computers by students with disabilities, approaches to get past those barriers, and applications of computing technology as compensatory strategies are easiest to identify and understand if we look at the limitations caused by various disabilities. The easiest way to recommend adaptive technology solutions is to work with limitations and tasks. First we identify the specific limitations a particular student has, and then we identify the tasks the individual is trying to accomplish.

Six main disability categories are used in this book in order to address particular problems that people have accessing and using computers and accomplishing other tasks that aren't usually performed on a computer:

- Vision impairments
- Mobility impairments
- Hearing impairments
- Learning disabilities
- Speech impairments
- Traumatic brain injuries

For our purposes, if a person has a vision impairment due to diabetes, approaches and strategies would be the same as if the vision disability were due to an injury or any other cause. Or, when we talk about people with mobility impairments that prohibit hand usage, we are concerned with how they can get access to computers or use computers as compensatory strategies, rather than why they can't use their hands. In some cases, people have both disabilities. In those instances, it becomes necessary to look at both the vision impairment category and the mobility impairment category to recommend possible adaptive strategies.

This is not a comprehensive training manual in how to assess the need for technology, how to prescribe technology, or how to use technology. Rather, this is a general overview of disability-related computer access needs and adaptive technology applications. We recommend that a professional with expertise in disabilities and assistive technology make recommendations on the types of approaches that are best for a particular student. We also recommend that students get clearances from their doctors, occupational therapists, or physical therapists before they use certain types of equipment.

Remember that approaches designed to overcome computer access barriers or to provide compensatory computer strategies will probably be used in conjunction with other assistance—such as tutors, interpreters, and readers.

COMPUTER ACCESS ISSUES

There are two potential computer access problems that exist for students with disabilities. The first is putting information into the computer (input), and the second is knowing what has been displayed on the monitor or has been printed by the computer printer (output). We will take a quick look at some of the adaptive technology that provides access for users with disabilities. Then we will suggest some of the ways in which this hardware and software can provide compensatory strategies to assist people with disabilities in accomplishing a wide variety of other tasks.

Computer Input Issues

Some people have trouble with the ordinary devices—the standard keyboard or mouse—used to input characters or commands into the computer. Generally, these input issues affect individuals who have limited or no control of hand movement. Input might also be a problem for students who have vision impairments or learning disabilities.

Mobility impairments include a large range of physical disabilities, from a sprained thumb to a condition in which a person has no control over his or her hands. Perhaps the finger most strained on the ordinary keyboard is the little finger on the right hand, which is forced to stretch frequently to strike the return key. Software that permits the user to redefine keys on the keyboard can help with some simple motor problems and may be useful in avoiding a repetitive stress injury. Some computer users find that ergonomic keyboards reduce such repetitive stress.

The Trace Research and Development Center has developed a public domain software, AccessDOS, that permits a user to avoid having to depress two keys simultaneously. This software also allows the user to alter the repeat rate, which is useful for people whose limited fine motor skills cause them to hold down a key for an unusually long period of time.

There are also a number of specialty keyboards to assist people with different mobility impairments. A membrane keyboard responds to a light touch and is beneficial for people who lack finger strength. Keyguards help keep computer users from depressing multiple keys inadvertently. Larger- or smaller-than-normal keyboards may facilitate some people's keyboard usage, and there are one-handed keyboards for people who only have the use of only one hand. The one-handed keyboard permits the user to depress several keys simultaneously. By using such keying techniques, users can input information into a computer without the use of a standard keyboard.

Manipulating a mouse is a problem for users with limited hand movement. Users who lack fine motor control in their hands also have problems with a standard mouse. A trackball frequently provides a good alternative. It can be manipulated with smaller motions than a mouse, and it is easier to control. There is also a type of software known as mouse keys that permits the use of arrow keys to move the mouse cursor around the screen. Mouse key software packages are available for both Macintosh and IBM-compatible computers.

There are still other adaptations for individuals who have no effective use of their hands. Some of these are simple and low tech, while others are more sophisticated and costly. Some mobility-impaired individuals depress the keys of a traditional keyboard with the use of a mouthstick. Others use a headwand, which is a pointer attached to a headband. Still others make do with a pencil held in the mouth. One person, who has shoulder movement but no finger movement, uses special Velcro gloves that he has made at a shoe repair shop. Unsharpened pencils are inserted into the gloves, and he uses the muscles in his shoulder to move his arm down and strike the keys with the pencils.

Most of these devices rely on head and neck motions to input data into the computer, so you must be sure that individuals using these types of adaptations take frequent rest breaks and consult with their doctors or rehabilitation consultants if problems occur.

Morse code is another input option for people with mobility impairments. One of the ways to produce Morse code without hand use is through a sip-and-puff straw. The sip-and-puff signals are created by the individual sipping (inhaling) or puffing (exhaling) into a straw, and these sips and puffs are translated through an interface device into the same electronic signals produced by depressing keys on the keyboard. The computer operates the same way as if the input had been through the keyboard. Morse code can be input by any device that can produce a binary signal—a representation of a dot and a dash. A simple set of switches positioned near a controllable muscle would produce a similar result. Again, with this type of adaptive device, be aware of the possibility that using the adaptive device could injure the person, and you should always consult with a doctor, physical therapist, or occupational therapist before recommending such a strategy.

Whether talking about traditional Morse code or adaptive computing uses of this code, skilled users can frequently achieve speeds between 30 and 40 words a minute, and there are ways to increase that rate significantly.

The on-screen keyboard is one of the more sophisticated input devices. A picture of the standard keyboard is displayed at the bottom of the computer monitor and is controlled by special adaptive software. In some cases, the user points at the key to be input. This may be done by a infrared device worn on the head that communicates with another infrared signal on the computer that does the pointing. Or, the computer could have the ability to "track" the gaze of the user's eyes and identify which on-screen key is being indicated. In another configuration, the software moves a blinking cursor across the on-screen keys until it reaches the one the user wants to input. At this point, by one of many devices, the user signals the computer to actually enter that data into the computer. The renowned physicist Stephen Hawking is only one of thousands of capable individuals who uses an on-screen keyboard system.

Many of these input systems are slow and tedious, so any way to speed them up is important. One of the useful tools for such users is word prediction software. As the user inputs the letters of a long word, the computer begins to guess what that word might be. When such predictions are tied to context or when the software has been "trained" to the user's vocabulary, word prediction can significantly increase the user's input rate.

The newest and most rapidly evolving alternative input system is voice recognition. Only a few years ago, voice recognition software cost many thousands of dollars and required users to talk very slowly with long, unnatural pauses between words. With newer technology, pauses are still important, but the user can speak more quickly and pause for a shorter time between words. When the software is trained to a user's speech patterns and pronunciation, the input rate approaches that of a skilled keyboard typist.

Voice recognition holds the promise of becoming a significant alternative input system for the computer. Because it has such broad appeal beyond the narrow market of disabled computer users, its price and quality will undoubtedly becoming increasingly attractive. A Boston law firm employs a lawyer who has limitations that make it impossible for her to use a standard keyboard for long periods of time. She uses voice recognition to connect to online legal databases and conducts extensive searches for the entire law firm. She uses a communications program to phone the databank and search engines to look for the legal information. She collects and packages the results of her searches in documents that can printed for the lawyer who requested the material.

Earlier we noted that some vision-impaired and learning-disabled individuals may have input difficulties as well. The adaptations that assist their input are identical to those they require for accessing computer output.

Computer Output Issues

Some people cannot access the computer's ordinary forms of output. They may have difficulty reading the screen due to vision impairments or learning disabilities. They may be unable to hear auditory cues, or they may have difficulty reading or handling a standard computer printout.

Individuals with low vision frequently benefit from an enlarged screen output. Being able to manipulate foreground and background colors is also useful. The ability to adjust the printer to produce documents in large type and to reformat the material to accommodate such enlargements is also important. These adaptations can also be useful to individuals with learning disabilities and various other cognitive processing problems. A cluttered display causes difficulties for both visual and mental processing.

The simplest approach for all computer users is to purchase a good-quality monitor with high resolution and sharp contrasts. Although they can be expensive, purchasing larger monitors may be all that is needed to provide adequate solutions for many people with low vision or learning disabilities.

Within the limitations of the standard computer, the adjustments for such disabilities are few. Adaptive software will permit enlarging the size of the letters and graphics on the screen by as much as 16 times. The Apple

Macintosh includes a utility, CloseView, which provides some enlargement. A good package for the Macintosh is inLARGE, and ZoomText is only one of several packages available for IBM-compatible computers.

Because the text displayed is enlarged, the original display will no longer fit entirely on the screen—the screen, in effect, becomes a window on the original display. The user moves around to find the desired information. When these systems are set for continuous reading, they handle the display of the material automatically, leaving the user free to concentrate on the content. An enlarged, uncluttered text helps many individuals concentrate and focus better on content.

At one large college library, such screen enlargement adaptations permit a vision-impaired staff member to supervise an adaptive technology lab. Besides handling the technical aspects of the computer, this technologist is in charge of training all students on the complete array of adaptive computer hardware and software that the library provides for its patrons. Having a person who uses adaptive devices involved in training students in the use of adaptive technology provides the students with a role model and with the encouragement that they, too, can join the workforce and participate in all aspects of society.

Synthetic speech is another alternative output system. It requires a speech synthesizer and specialized screen-reading software. Synthetic speech enables people who have no vision to get output from a computer. Synthetic speech may also be useful to individuals with learning disabilities who learn better by hearing information than by reading it.

Speech synthesizers work with phonetics and sounds, not with words as such. If they worked with words, the software driving the synthesizer would have to scour a large dictionary to find each word and then be given instructions on that word's proper pronunciation. Instead, speech synthesizers function with highly complex sets of rules of phonetics. English is far from being a genuinely phonetic language, however, which sometimes results in confusing, and frequently amusing, pronunciations of words. What can a synthesizer do with *cough, rough,* or *dough?* Generally, the better the quality of the synthesizer and screen-reading software, the more rules there are and the more likely that the pronunciation will be correct. The earlier and less expensive systems also tended to sound the most mechanical and have the least intonations. Until these systems include enough artificial intelligence to have some grasp of the context for the words they are speaking, we can assume that the speech synthesizer will be reading in a mechanical voice. People generally become accustomed to it, and some even find that the flat voice allows them to set the equipment to an extremely high rate of speed.

The screen-reading software that functions with a synthesizer is important. The software must do more than merely capture the text going to the screen and send it simultaneously to the synthesizer. People with normal vision are able to scan a document they are reading, and a good screen-reading software program should offer similar options to people using synthetic speech. For example, pretend you are shown a menu of 10 choices, one at a time, and a second after each item appears, it disappears. Which item did you want? When a menu appears on a traditional computer monitor, the eye scans it quickly and then flicks back over a couple items as you make your decision. This all happens so fast that you are not aware of reading and rereading the screen. Blind computer users need to be able to do the same thing. Screen-reading software permits the user to move an audible cursor around the screen, which rereads what the synthesizer has already spoken. When the user is confused or needs more detail, the software must permit reading the material a line, a word, or a character at a time. While the user may normally listen to the speech synthesizer with the punctuation feature turned off, sometimes knowing punctuation is crucial to comprehension, and the computer user will need to be able to control volume and speed, as well as other speech attributes.

Listening to material on a computer screen means that items are normally presented line by line, from left to right. When the display contains material in columns, the listener can be confused. Good software permits the user to identify columns and read by columns. Other material uses colors, flashing letters, and reverse displays to convey special meaning. Again, the screen-reading software must be able to interpret such meaning for the user.

Refreshable Braille is another way for blind users to gain access to a computer display. A device attached to the computer keyboard contains small pins that can be rapidly raised and lowered to make Braille characters. It normally presents one line of data either 40 or 80 characters long and essentially is a tactile window providing access to a portion of the monitor. The user can move around this refreshable Braille "window" to gain access to the entire screen. This provides an accurate representation of the display content, whereas words spoken by a speech synthesizer can be misunderstood, and numbers are hard to manipulate aurally. Many blind programmers find the degree of reliability offered by refreshable Braille essential for their work, though it is relatively expensive.

Braille embossers function like a standard printer, though the paper must be heavier and the embossing can be noisy. Some embossers produce output with Braille on both sides of the page. To make use of a Braille embosser, the user must take the word processor file and run it through a special translation program. This does several things. It will usually translate the text into Grade II Braille, which is a type of shorthand. The translation program also must reformat pages because the normal Braille page is only 40 characters wide. Taking a standard literary text file and outputting a Braille document is normally straightforward, with the hard work being done by the translation software. This means that someone knowing no Braille can produce Braille documents for blind students.

Finally, optical scanners and optical character recognition (OCR) software are important tools for blind individuals, especially students and professionals. A scanner, of course, is not an output device. Its function is to provide a direct way to input data into a computer without having to re-key it. Blind users, too, may use it in this way. For a blind user, however, getting text from paper into the computer may really only be the first step toward displaying that text on the monitor and through the synthesizer. Most people wanting to read a paper document will pick up the text and read it. For a blind person, the computer replaces a human reader, and the blind individual's interest in the scanner is as a means toward displaying the text in an accessible format.

COMPUTERS AS COMPENSATORY TOOLS

Students using computing hardware and software as compensatory tools might be trying to accomplish tasks such as reading, writing, organizing information, researching information, taking tests, and communicating.

Basic Tasks

Reading

In the past, students who were blind, had low vision, or were otherwise unable to handle printed material were dependent on other people to read their assignments to them. Now they can use an optical character reader that reads through a speech synthesizer. The student can also produce ASCII files and read by reviewing the material on a computer screen or through a speech synthesizer. A blind student can scan material into a computer and then use a Braille embosser to print it out in Braille. This strategy is particularly useful when writing a research paper; the student can print out and proofread the paper in Braille, make corrections, and then print a regular paper copy for the professor.

Writing

A student who has a disability that affects hand usage might have the services of a note taker or transcriber. An alternate strategy would be for the student to use a laptop computer and input device to take notes in the class and then print them out in either normal or large-type print. The student could also review the notes online. Or, a blind student can use a laptop to take notes in class and then later read them with the use of a speech synthesizer. In these cases, it is quite possible that the student's use of the laptop computer would cost the school less than a note taker for each student. Students with vision or mobility impairments would also want to use adapted computers to produce written assignments. Such students would benefit from keyboard performance enhancement programs such as abbreviation expansion or word prediction.

Organizing Information

Students, especially those with learning disabilities, would benefit from outlining software that helps organize information more efficiently, both for study and for producing written assignments.

Researching Information

Students with print handicaps (generally those individuals who have vision or mobility impairments) benefit from the use of online information. Most libraries now have digitized catalogs, databases on CD-ROM, electronic journals, a few electronic books, and accessible computers to allow disabled students to research the material they need. Most books are still not available electronically, although organizations such as Recording for the Blind and Dyslexic are making audio and electronic versions of many publications (see Chapter 10).

Taking Tests

Students who are blind or have low vision may need a speech synthesizer to hear the questions, enter their answers, and then verify them with a screen-reading program. Some low-vision students may need a screen enlarger or magnification accommodation. A learning-disabled student may need a computerized spelling checker or the use of a screen-reading program and a speech synthesizer. (See King and Jarrow, *Testing Accommodations*.)

Communicating

Many campuses use computerized phone systems for registration and to give information on grades and student status. Students with hearing or physical impairments would need compensatory strategies to give them equal access to all such communication systems. Hearing-impaired students might benefit from the use of a TTY, while mobility-impaired students may need the use of a speech synthesizer or other output device.

Equipment Commonly Used by Blind People

Braille Embosser and Printer

Braille printers emboss information for reading by a blind person who reads Braille. Prior to printing, a conversion to Grade II Braille—a contraction technique that reduces the number of characters—is advisable. Most people who read Braille prefer Grade II because it takes less paper and is faster to read. The conversion to Grade II does require an extra processing step, however, with Braille translation software.

Braille Key Labels

These can be created by using a DynaTape device and are useful in establishing relative key positions. It is unlikely that a person who uses Braille would be able to read the letters with all fingers sitting directly on top of the keys, as Braille is read by moving the fingers across raised dots. However, Braille DynaTape is useful for identifying many keys on the keyboard that may vary from keyboard to keyboard, such as the *Ctrl* key and *Delete*. Clear DynaTape allows a sighted user to still be able to read the key labels.

Laptop Computer

A laptop computer with adaptive input tools and word abbreviation or word prediction software helps people achieve the fastest possible data-entry rate. Also use a voice synthesizer with screen-reading software to have notes read back later.

Online Information

Materials that are online will be available to individuals with the appropriate adapted equipment mentioned previously. Arrangements must be made with libraries to provide printed materials in an accessible format. Adapted computers should be available in libraries for access to electronic catalogs and CD-ROMs. It might also be necessary to provide an optical character reader to convert printed material to electronic media that can then be provided on a diskette for a person to read at his or her own computer. It may be necessary for libraries to contact the Library of Congress to determine if printed material is available on cassette tape for the use of a person with a disability. (This technique is useful for people with any type of disability, and of course, for people without disabilities, as well).

Optical Character Recognition (OCR) Reader

A "reading machine" or "personal reader" can scan a printed document and convert the information to sound. The device has a built-in speech synthesizer to convert the scanned document to synthetic speech. Units are fairly expensive ($8,000 to $12,000), but they give immediate access to printed material.

Refreshable Braille Display (RBD)

This will display information in increments of 20, 40, or 80 Braille characters at a time. Navigation around the screen is provided by keys of the RBD. Braille information is displayed on a strip-type device that normally sits directly in front of the standard computer keyboard so that hand movement between the keyboard and the display is minimized.

Graphical User Interface (GUI)

The advent of the graphical user interface a few years ago turned out to be a mixed blessing for people with disabilities. While many people with learning disabilities, some people with mobility impairments, and deaf people found GUI to be helpful, computer users who are blind and some mobility-impaired people found this new interface to be an insurmountable barrier. GUI puts information on the screen using different technical methods than did the traditional DOS machines. Screen readers were confronted with pictures of letters and groupings of pixels, and they could not interpret the information.

The problem with adaptive computing is that the programmers are adapting systems after they have been built. They are always playing catch-up. Gradually, screen-reading software that could provide spoken output for GUI began to appear. However, the GUI display itself has a visual orientation which is harder for blind users to understand and manipulate. The first screen reader was OutSpoken for Macintosh. Several Windows screen readers followed. But at that very moment, Windows 95 was poised for release, and the game of catch-up began all over again. Screen readers for Windows 95 first appeared in the fall of 1996. Early reports are that the systems are more stable and dependable than previous ones. Also, many blind users find the new display to be simpler and easier to use.

Earlier in 1996, Microsoft hired several programmers and systems analysts to design their operating system to be more accessible to software designed for users with disabilities. There is hope that more access will become part of the system itself and not require as much adaptation. The modern computer is fast enough and has enough memory to permit the design of programs with user-definable interfaces.

Screen-Reading Systems

These systems speak the information being shown on a computer screen. The systems include a speech synthesizer and a screen reading software program. The speech synthesizer is a device that converts ASCII texts to spoken output. The screen reading software allows the user to direct what portion of the screen should be processed through the synthesizer. They vary in price and quality.

There are several screen reading systems that will make computers accessible to people who are blind or have low vision. Carl Brown, director of the High-Tech Center for the Disabled, part of the California Community Colleges Chancellor's Office, describes important features in screen reading systems (see Brown, "Computer Access," 1.4–1.7):

- Straightforward to use (as much as possible).
- Cost effective (be sure to consider cost effectiveness in concert with overall effectiveness; if the text enlargement program does not operate in the spelling checker, additional staff support will be required to help the visually impaired person complete a task).
- Works with both text and graphics.
- Works with a monochrome, color, or enhanced color display.
- Works with a variety of voice synthesizers.
- Works with standard word processing, spreadsheet, and database programs.
- Allows automatic, adjustable scrolling of text.
- Reads any portion of the screen, including letters, words, lines, and sentences.
- Provides spoken output of spaces, punctuation, ASCII values, prompts, and messages, and the military version of letters.
- Identifies format of the text.
- Automatically reads error messages.
- Compatible with local area network or terminal emulation.
- Has documentation available in print, audiotape, Braille, or on floppy disk.

Equipment Commonly Used by People with Low Vision and Learning Disabilities

These strategies are more useful for a person with low vision, rather than a blind person. Any of the adaptive devices recommended for blind people might also be useful. These accommodations are also good for people with learning disabilities due to visual acuity problems.

Altered Colors on a Monitor

Colors can be changed from a black background and white foreground to a white background and black foreground, or to some other color combination that is found to be helpful. Some word processing and character magnification programs offer color control as a standard feature.

Anti-Glare Screen

This removes light reflection or glare from a monitor screen.

Closed-Circuit Television (CCTV)

This will help enlarge text. Use of the camera feature will magnify printed materials up to 60 times.

Copy Holder with Guides

Sometimes something as simple as a ruler or paper guide will aid people in finding and reading information on printed copy. Some copy holders have a guide for keeping a place on the document being used.

Enlarged Cursor

This will help a person who has difficulty seeing the standard one-sixteenth-inch, flat-type cursor. The enlarged cursor is normally a software function.

Font Sizes and Styles

Changing type sizes and fonts may be helpful. This is a function of some word processing programs. Pixel density can be a issue, especially when information is magnified by a screen-magnification program, a large monitor, or a CCTV. Some magnification programs display information in a jagged form, while others have a more contoured shape. You also should experiment to find a large type size to print information.

Hardware-Assisted Magnification

This normally requires a card inside the computer and may use a mouse to control character size and navigation around the screen. Having to insert a card in the system lessens the flexibility and portability. The advantage is in the ability to navigate around the screen and locate information more quickly than with a software-only solution.

Highlighted Portions of Text

This simple technique may make reading easier for some people.

Large Monitor

Seventeen-inch to 21-inch monitors are helpful to many individuals with low vision who don't need the larger magnification provided by large-print software. They offer a full-screen image.

One Word or One Line on the Monitor at a Time

Too much information displayed at one time may make it difficult for people with certain types of vision impairments and learning disabilities. Some screen-magnification programs and closed-circuit televisions offer this option.

Screen-Magnifying Lens

This is a magnifying piece of plastic or glass that sits directly in front of the monitor. By moving it farther away from the monitor, the information will be magnified. Maximum enlargement is about two to three times. This solution may be sufficient for some users and is the least expensive magnification option. With this option, the whole screen can be viewed at one time.

Software Programs to Magnify Text or Graphics

Normally called terminate-and-stay-resident or TSR programs, these will only be active when specifically requested and can be deactivated when not required. Magnification will normally range from 2 to 16 times the regular character size. Using software gives good flexibility and portability by allowing a person to use any computer by merely loading the magnification program. The size of magnification controls how much information is displayed at one time. If a 2 percent magnification is selected, only 40 characters across and 12 lines down a screen will be visible at a time. Through scrolling or cursor movement, the balance of the screen can be viewed. With 8 percent magnification, only 10 horizontal characters can be viewed with 3 vertical lines.

Wide or Narrow Margins

Experiment with margins and line widths. This is a function of a word processing program. Too much information spread across too wide a space may be a problem to some visually-impaired and learning-disabled people.

Equipment Commonly Used by People with Mobility Impairments

The equipment listed here is also helpful for people with learning disabilities.

Disks

Use floppy disks that are able to withstand fairly rough handling. They should be hard-cased to accept light clamping. Most floppy disks today meet that criterion. Only the older 5.25-inch diskettes would be a problem. Try to shield all diskettes from liquid spills, crimping, and exposure to excessive heat or electromagnetic fields.

When the computer ejects diskettes, they should protrude 0.75 to 1.5 inches for ease of removal by a person with limited hand or arm capabilities or who might be using a hand prosthesis with clamps or grippers.

Diskette guides are available to aid in the insertion of a diskette. They mount at a slightly downward angle to aid in guiding the diskette into the drive opening. Media should be front loading and should unload by push-button or program ejection.

Keyboards

Special keyboards can provide larger or smaller target areas. An enlarged keyboard may have key sizes that are two to four times the size of keys on a standard keyboard. The keying areas are normally pressure sensitive so that the user can slide his or her hand across they keyboard until he or she reaches the desired key and then apply enough pressure to have the character entered, just like depressing a key on a regular keyboard. The mini-keyboard might be as small as seven inches wide and four inches high. It may be necessary to use a pointer or pencil to press keys due to the compactness of the key layout. Both the enlarged and miniature keyboards are normally programmable so that the keys can be changed to place the most frequently used keys closer together, minimizing the amount of movement required to reach them. A membrane keyboard is flat surface. Like the keyguard, it allows the hands to slide across the surface. Then pressure is applied to the appropriate key to cause character entry.

Keyguards

Keyguards are pieces of plastic or metal that fit over keyboards. They have holes drilled or molded directly above each key. By using a finger, pointer, or mouthstick, a person can press only one key at a time. This can be useful to a person with cerebral palsy, a hand tremor, or spastic hand movement. The keyguard can be attached to the keyboard by clips or Velcro so that it is easily removed.

Laptop Computers

Use a laptop computer with adaptive input tools, such as word abbreviation or word prediction software, to achieve the fastest possible data-entry rate. Tools that an individual might use in a lab, such as switches, may also be required for use with a laptop in the classroom for note taking.

Limb Rests

Supporting hands and arms with rests may help some individuals. Additionally, it may be beneficial to move a keyboard from its usual position in front of the computer. For example, for a person with no arms, the keyboard can be placed on the floor and the keys can be depressed with toes or a pointer attached to the leg. For a person in a wheelchair, it may be necessary to place the keyboard on the person's lap or on the tray of the chair.

Mechanical Key-Locking Devices

These can be positioned over one or more of the keys that need to be pressed. When lowered into "lock position," a single finger, mouthstick, or headpointer can be used to press the final key for the multi-key sequence. Then the locking device can be raised and pushed away from the keyboard until needed again. AccessDOS for PCs and Easy Access for Macs are free key-locking software. Contact the Trace Research and Development Center for information (see Appendix B).

On-Screen Keyboards, Coupled with the Following

Scanning Software and Switches This software uses a "row-column scan" technique that highlights a row of letters on a keyboard pictured on the screen. After a set interval of time, the next row of letters will be highlighted. When the row that contains the character that the user wants is highlighted, the user presses a switch and the program highlights the characters across the row, one at a time. When the character the user wants is highlighted, he presses the switch again to select and enter it. This process is repeated to build words, sentences, and complete documents. This may appear to be slow—but when used with word-prediction or abbreviation programs, a fairly good rate of data entry can be achieved.

Optical Headpointers/Ultrasonic Headpointers By aiming the optical headpointer at an on-screen keyboard for a preselected amount of time, the character indicated will be entered. This becomes a one-step process (as opposed to the two steps used by the row-column scan program). The ultrasonic headpointer operates on the same principle as an optical headpointer. It is a direct-select process that gives good data-entry speed.

Mouse, Joystick, or Trackball These devices can be used to point an on-screen arrow or pointer at the desired character on the on-screen keyboard. Clicking the device while it is on the desired character will enter the character. Note that a mouse and a trackball share the same connection on a computer but may require different supporting software. A joystick requires a special card on most computers and will have its own supporting software. Do not expect to connect a joystick through a mouse connection port.

Word Prediction Software Word prediction software takes any character entered from the keyboard and looks it up in its program dictionary. The program will display a selection box with a list of the most likely words or phrases that begin with that character. The list may have one to five or more words or phrases displayed with the most likely word or phrase at the top of the list. If the word or phrase wanted is on the list, the individual would use directional arrows on the keyboard to highlight the desired word or phrase and press *Enter* or click a mouse to enter the word or phrase. If the word or phrase is not in the selection box, the user enters another character and a new list of words or phrases is displayed that begin with the characters entered. This process is repeated until the correct word or phrase appears or the word is completely spelled without appearing on the list. Normally a program of this type will keep track of the frequency of word use and adjust the list of words or phrases displayed on the selection box.

Abbreviation Expansion Software Abbreviation expansion software takes characters entered, looks them up in the program dictionary, and when it finds a combination of characters that matches an abbreviation in the dictionary, the expansion of the word or phrase is entered. Abbreviations may expand to a word, phrase, sentence, paragraph, or a whole document. If you are familiar with the Gregg Shorthand method, this is very similar. Various dictionaries are available for normal use or for medical, legal, insurance, COBOL, or specialized vocabularies. A user can also add words, names, and phrases to customize the program. For repetitive, form letter-type correspondence, an individual may achieve the equivalent of entering several hundred words per minute. This makes the mouthstick and switches previously mentioned reasonable solutions for people who need some level of data entry performance.

Rearrangement or "Remapping"

Key locations on the keyboard can be rearranged by a software program that places the most frequently used keys closer together to improve key performance. This minimizes the time to move a single finger or pointer across the entire keyboard, from the A key to the P key. There are both left- and right-hand versions of the "remapping" of key locations.

Sip-and-Puff Devices Used with Morse Code

The use of dots and dashes has proven useful for people with limited or no hand use. A sip-and-puff device can be used along with a teletype switch or a simple open-close type circuit device. A software program to convert the dots and dashes to keyboard equivalent characters is available. Most people using Morse code can reach speeds of 15–30 words per minute. This could be an improvement for a person who is using a single finger or pointing device.

Sticky-Key Software

These software programs allow an individual to press each key separately in a multiple-key operation. For example, a person can press Ctrl, then Alt, then Delete, sequentially, to reboot a system, instead of the usual method of holding down the Ctrl and Alt keys while Delete is pressed. If a person using a single finger, a mouthstick, or a headpointer wants to type a capital letter, he or she can press Shift and then the letter. That letter will be capitalized and all following letters will be in lower case. Pressing the Shift key twice will lock into upper case, and all letters will be typed as capitals until the key is pressed again, which returns the keyboard to the lower case mode. Sticky keys are standard on Macintosh computers.

Switches

Position controls at the front edge of the computer, and use a power strip to provide a single source to turn on all electrical devices. The power strip should be positioned where it would be easily reachable with a mouthstick, headpointer, or a single finger. Also try using sliding or edge-operated controls; control buttons or levers that operate in up-down or lateral fashions; double-acting, push-button controls; and rocker-type switches with concave surfaces so that mouthsticks, headpointers, or arm-brace pointers have an easy surface to push against.

Select switches or controls that require less pressure than is usually required to manipulate computers. The companies that manufacture switches can tell you the amount of pressure that is required to operate a switch. If an individual cannot generate 100 grams of pressure, then look for another switch with less pressure required, or find a company that can provide a switch to meet an individual's capability.

Trackballs and Joysticks

Try a trackball, which is similar to an upside-down mouse, in which the user rotates the ball to control the movement of the pointer on the screen. There are buttons on the trackball that simulate the clicking functions of a mouse. A joystick, which looks like a pistol-grip or a device that might be on the controls of an arcade-type game, can perform the same function.

Typing Sticks

Various kinds of sticks are used to depress keys on a keyboard. A mouthstick is a lightweight stick—wooden, plastic, or metal. It attaches to a mouthpiece that resembles a dental upper plate. The stick is used to press keys on the keyboard. The keyboard is normally positioned at an angle so the stick can be pointed directly into a key. Many people with limited or no hand movement use a variety of devices to depress keys. Don't overlook something as simple as pencils inserted into special gloves. This solution works quite well for people who have shoulder movement, but no hand or finger movement or strength.

Voice Recognition

Voice recognition uses a microphone with a software program and a computer card to input information and perform computer control through voice utterances or speech. The use of this tool normally requires training the system to recognize the voice pattern of the user. The more the person uses the program, the more accurately the program performs. This would be useful to a person with limited or no hand use, such as a person with cerebral palsy or a spinal cord injury. It may also be useful for certain types of learning disabilities.

Equipment Commonly Used by People with Hearing Impairments

Headphones

If the computer has a jack for a headphone, use a headphone with whatever amplification the individual can hear. Headphones can also be used when a person is learning a word processing or database program and listening to an audiocassette instruction tape.

Hearing Loops

Also called induction loops, these are loops of wire that go around a room—either under the carpet or on the ceiling—and are connected to amplifiers. A hearing-loop with remote sound transmission works well for some people who use hearing aids. These would also be helpful if the computer lab adaptive computing specialist is conducting group classes with a hearing impaired individual.

Icons and Flashing Screens

Use a software program that will convert auditory signals to display a flashing screen, a specific icon, or a picture of a musical note in place of an audible signal. The user must be on the lookout to recognize the signal and take appropriate action. Norton Utilities on Macintosh shows an icon when disk drives are operational. IBM PS/2s and later models have a visual indicator that shows when drives are in use. Clones may vary, and a utility may be required for icon verification.

Telecommunication Devices for the Deaf (TDD) TeleTYpewriters (TTYs or TTs)

TDDs and TTYs are ideal for people with hearing impairments, but not all schools and businesses have the appropriate equipment. The communications provision of ADA Title IV mandated that as of July 26, 1993, telephone companies had to provide a relay service for a person who is hearing or speech impaired. While this is a nice service, it requires a third party to act as the go-between, and privacy becomes an issue when personal and confidential matters are discussed.

Equipment That Is Useful to Individuals with Learning Disabilities

Spell-checking software, online dictionaries and thesauruses, abbreviation expansion software, and word prediction software can all be useful tools for individuals with learning disabilities. However, all of these tools must be used in a way that the individual learns from their usage, rather than trying to use these tools as a replacement for his or her own skills.

Voice Recognition Systems

Voice recognition systems might be helpful to people with spelling difficulties because voice recognition systems incorporate a dictionary into the recognition process. Also, some people with learning disabilities can think better if they express thoughts aloud.

Outlining Programs

There are a number of outlining programs on the market today which are used quite successfully by both people with disabilities and those without disabilities to process ideas, organize thoughts, and arrange material to be more easily understood. These programs provide flexibility, but they're useless unless the individual knows how to outline in the first place. They should initially be used in a tutorial environment so the individual can get assistance in learning outlining skills.

CHAPTER

Matching People and Technology

This practical chapter lists specific disability-related barriers or difficulties followed by approaches or strategies that can help in overcoming them.

VISION IMPAIRMENTS

Because this category includes low vision, functional vision, color blindness, and blindness, the spectrum of computer access approaches and compensatory strategies must offer several choices. In this section, we'll look at approaches and strategies for people who are blind and people who have low vision. General barriers to computer access include the inability to read computer screens, to see keys on standard keyboards, and to orient on the keyboard.

Computer Access Approaches for Individuals Who Are Blind

Sighted people use a variety of techniques when they produce text with a computer. They can quickly review information at any location on the computer screen. A quick glance, for example, will indicate a typing error. They edit their text as they type, checking their spelling, grammar, and logic. They are also able to format their text by viewing options on a program menu, examining a systems prompt, or selecting an option. In order to make computers accessible to blind individuals, technology must provide a non-visual method for "seeing" the screen. This can be accomplished in two ways, auditory and tactile.

Barrier   Individual can't see the keys on a computer keyboard.
Approaches
- Use locator dots on keys.
- Use a screen-reading program that announces each key depression.

Barrier   Individual can't see text on the computer monitor.
Approaches
- Use screen-reading software (e.g., Jaws and Vert) and a speech synthesizer (e.g., DECtalk, Accent, and Artic Business Vision).
- Use a refreshable Braille display (e.g., Navigator).

Barrier   Individual cannot read computer printouts.
Approaches
- Use a Braille embosser and printer for document creation (e.g., Romeo Braille).
- Use a screen-reading program with a speech synthesizer.
- Use a refreshable Braille display.
- Use an optical character recognition reading system.

Compensatory Strategies for Individuals Who Are Blind

Difficulty   Individual has difficulty reading or proofreading printed materials (such as tests, books, registration materials, catalogs, and research materials).
Strategies
- Use an optical character recognition (OCR)/reading machine (e.g., Arkenstone and Kurzweil Personal Reader) with a screen reader and a speech synthesizer.
- Use a Braille embosser to produce printouts.
- Use online research and registration materials (e.g., an encyclopedia on CD-ROM or materials available in computer-readable format) that can be accessed through screen readers and speech synthesizers.

Difficulty   Individual has difficulty taking notes in class, taking exams, and producing written assignments.
Strategies
- Use a laptop computer with adaptive devices in the classroom.
- Use a computer to take tests and produce written assignments.

Computer Access Approaches for Individuals with Low Vision

One problem for people with low vision is that the text display on the normal computer screen is too small to be easily read. Another problem is that many individuals can't see the keys on the keyboard satisfactorily. Certain screen color combinations can also cause problems for individuals who are color blind, individuals with low vision, and individuals with learning disabilities.

Barrier   Individual can't clearly see the keys on a keyboard.
Approaches
- Use key caps with large or relief letters or locator dots.
- Use a screen-reading program that announces each key depression.

Barrier   Individual has limited view of text on monitor due to size or color, or individual has difficulty finding place on screen.
Approaches
- Use an anti-glare screen.
- Change the color on the monitor.
- Use an enlarged cursor.
- Experiment with different font sizes and styles.
- Put only one word or line of text on the monitor at a time.
- Highlight portions of text.
- Use software to magnify text or graphics.
- Use hardware-assisted magnifications.
- Use a screen-magnifying lens.
- Use a large monitor.
- Use a screen-reading program and speech synthesizer.

Barrier   Individual can't read usual computer printouts or has trouble finding his or her place on copy.
Approaches
- Use a copy holder with line guides.
- Use wider or smaller margins and line widths.
- Use closed-circuit television to view printed text.
- Use software to enlarge text of printout, such as NicePrint or Power Pak.
- Use a Braille embosser to create documents.
- Use a screen-reading program with a speech synthesizer.
- Use an optical character recognition reading system.

Compensatory Strategies for Individuals with Low Vision

Difficulty   Individual has problems reading and proofreading printed materials (e.g., tests, books, registration materials, catalogs, and research materials).
Strategies
- Convert materials to computer-readable format and use one of the following approaches for reading information from a computer screen: software to enlarge text of printout (e.g., NicePrint, Power Pak, and large base fonts from Macintosh); optical character recognition (OCR)/ reading machines (e.g., Arkenstone, Kurzweil Personal Reader, and Oscar) with screen-reading program (e.g., Vert and Jaws) and speech

synthesizer (e.g., DECtalk, Keynote Gold, Artic Business Vision, and Accent).

- Use a closed-circuit television to enlarge print and graphics.
- Use a Braille embosser to produce printouts.
- Use online research materials (e.g., an encyclopedia on CD-ROM) and online registration materials and catalogs.

Difficulty Individual has problems producing (and proofreading) printed assignments.

Strategies

- Use software to enlarge text of printout.
- Use a Braille embosser to produce Braille version for proofing.

MOBILITY IMPAIRMENTS

There are many mobility impairments that can make computer use difficult. Individuals with mobility impairments include people with congenital disabilities, spinal cord injuries, progressive neuralgic diseases, and people who are without the use of hands, arms, or legs. The impairments that are addressed in this chapter relate primarily to limited or no hand usage. Mobility impairments that are experienced by people in wheelchairs are generally access to the computer lab or building, and they are addressed in Chapter 5.

The primary computer access barriers for individuals with hand-usage impairment involve computer input devices and the handling of storage media and paper output. Additionally, people with these particular mobility disabilities often have difficulty writing down information, producing written documents, and holding items such as books. There are many compensatory strategies that can be effectively used by people with mobility impairments, but *it is absolutely imperative that an evaluation be made by a qualified physical therapist or occupational therapist before any adaptive equipment is used for a student with a mobility impairment.* There is a risk of causing physical injury to a student, and therefore, there is also a risk of litigation.

Computer Access Approaches for Individuals with Hand-Usage Impairment

People with no hand use will have some of the following problems using a computer.

Barrier Individual can't use a standard keyboard.

Approaches

- Use a mouthstick, headwand (headpointer), typing stick, or other device to press keys. (Note: Be sure to consult with an occupational or physical therapist for advice on selecting the appropriate device.)

- Use keyguards.
- Use enlarged or miniature keyboards.
- Use a voice recognition systems such as DragonDictate, VoiceType, or VoiceWord.
- Use an on-screen keyboard coupled with such devices as: scanning software and adaptive switch (e.g., sip and puff); optical headpointer (e.g., Freeboard); ultrasonic headpointer (e.g., HeadMaster); or a mouse, joystick, or trackball.
- Use Morse code input with a sip-and-puff device or switches.
- Position body for maximum use of an individual's "controllable anatomical site." (Note: Only a person trained in physical disabilities and/or body positioning should make such recommendations. Services at a seating clinic are covered by Medicaid, Medicare, and some other types of insurance.)

Two additional approaches enhance most of the above-mentioned access approaches:

- Word prediction software (increases production rate if used in conjunction with a scanning program or on-screen keyboard with optical headpointer/ultrasonic headpointer; e.g., KeyWiz, Access 190, and Handikey).
- Abbreviation expansion software (increases production rate if used in conjunction with a scanning program or on-screen keyboard with optical headpointer/ultrasonic headpointer; e.g., KeyWiz).

Barrier   Individual can't press keys simultaneously (e.g., *Shift* and a letter key for capitalization).
Approaches
- Use "sticky key" software to "latch" keys so that key combination can be done sequentially by one finger, headwand, or mouthstick (e.g., AccessDOS, which is available from IBM at no cost).
- Use a mechanical key-locking device.

Barrier   Individual has a slowed rate of typing or typing inaccuracy, can't quickly release keys, and/or is unable to access all keys on a standard keyboard.
Approaches
- Reposition computer equipment to improve accuracy.
- Use wrist rests or arm rests.
- Use keyguards.
- Rearrange keyboard layout.
- Use an enlarged keyboard, miniature keyboard, membrane keyboard, or other type of nonstandard keyboard.
- Use software to control key entry and repeat rates.

- Use a sip-and-puff device with Morse code.
- Use an optical pointing device with an on-screen keyboard (such as Freeboard and Freewheel or HeadMaster), with word prediction or abbreviation expansion software.
- Use scanning software with word prediction or abbreviation expansion (e.g., Access 190).
- Use a voice recognition system.

Two additional approaches enhance most of the above-mentioned access approaches:
- Word prediction software (e.g., KeyWiz, Access 190, and Handikey).
- Abbreviation expansion software (e.g., KeyWiz).

Barrier   Individual can't use mouse or graphics pad.
Approaches
- Use keyboard commands for mouse functions (e.g., T-TAM).
- Use a trackball or joystick instead of a mouse.
- Use voice recognition.

Computer Access Approaches for Individuals with Limited Motion, Strength, and Coordination

People with limited range of motion, strength, or fine motor control and poor coordination have slower or irregular reaction times, making time-dependent computer input difficult.

Barrier   Individual is unable to operate switches or controls located at the rear of the computer.
Approaches
- Locate controls at the front edge of the equipment (e.g., an on-off switch attached to the power supply).

Barrier   Individual is unable to use latches or controls that require twist motion (e.g., disk drive door latches, monitor control knobs).
Approaches
- Use sliding or edge-operated controls.
- Use up-down control buttons.
- Use double-acting, push-button controls.
- Use concave rocker switches.

Barrier   Individual cannot open laptop computers with double latches that require simultaneous release.
Approach
- Use laptop computers with latches that can be opened sequentially.

Barrier   Individual is unable to operate controls that require much force (more than 100 grams).
Approaches
- Use push-button controls requiring less than 100 grams of pressure.
- Use an optical or ultrasonic headpointer with an on-screen keyboard program to operate controls.

Barriers   Individual can't type accurately, press keys simultaneously, press only one key at a time, quickly release keys, access all of the keys on a standard keyboard, or use a mouse.
Approaches
- See approaches from previous sections.
- Use wrist rests or elbow rests to increase stability. (Note: Be sure to obtain the advice of an expert before selecting a device for any individual.)

Barriers   Individual has problems reaching built-in drives, especially on floor-mount computers, and/or difficulty reaching into disk drives to remove floppy disks, CD-ROMs, and other media.
Approaches
- Use media drives that are external to the computer and can be moved to allow insertion and removal with minimal reach and manual dexterity.
- Use diskette guides to assist in inserting and removing floppy disks.
- Use removable media that ejects and/or protrudes a minimum of 0.75 to 1.5 inches from the drive.
- Use media and drives that are self-guiding and that load and unload from the front by push-button or software ejection.
- Use ejection buttons that are concave rather than flat (they are easier to operate with a mouthstick or headwand).

Barrier   Individual has difficulty inserting disks without damaging them.
Approaches
- Use removable media that is able to withstand fairly rough handling; it should be hard-cased to accept light clamping.
- Use diskette guides to assist in inserting and removing media.

Compensatory Strategies for Individuals with Mobility Impairments

Computers can be used in nontraditional ways to enable people with mobility impairments to accomplish tasks that would otherwise be difficult or impossible. The primary difficulties are in writing down information and producing written documents. The following strategies allow individuals with mobility impairments to use computers to accomplish those tasks.

Difficulty   Individual has trouble holding a pen for making notes, writing in-class assignments, and taking tests.
Strategy
   • Use laptop computer and adaptive input device for taking class notes and tests, and for producing homework assignments.

Difficulty   Individual has difficulty handling library research materials.
Strategy
   • Use online research materials accessible with adaptive interface to retrieve materials.

HEARING IMPAIRMENTS

Individuals in this group may be hearing impaired, or they may be deaf. These individuals may have difficulty hearing auditory output from computers, or they may not be allowed to turn up the volume sufficiently due to environmental constraints. Some general tips: Adjust the computer volume controls to be as loud as possible (but not so loud that the sound disturbs others working in the area) and limit noise in the environment.

   People who are hearing impaired or deaf currently have little difficulty using computers; however, as computers increasingly rely on auditory cues, access barriers are actually being built in for people with hearing impairments. Visual redundancy of auditory clicks and tones would address most of the problems in this area. The primary concern is to ensure that future audible information is provided in a visually redundant form.

Computer Access Approaches for Individuals with Hearing Impairments

Barrier   Individual has difficulty hearing beeps that indicate errors when typing or issuing commands.
Approaches (for hearing impaired, rather than deaf individuals)
   • Adjust volume appropriately.
   • Place individuals in quiet environments and reduce extraneous sounds as much as possible. For example, don't place a hearing impaired individual near a loud fan.
   • Use headphones with adjustable volume.
   • Use hearing loops with remote sound transmission.

- For both hearing impaired and deaf individuals, replace auditory signals with a flashing screen or icons (e.g., See Beep for IBM compatibles; set volume control to zero on Macintosh computers).

Barrier   Individual is unable to turn the volume up sufficiently in some settings such as libraries or noisy environments.
Approach
- Use headphones (hearing loops with remote sound transmission work well for some people who use hearing aids).

Barrier   Individual can't hear warning beeps and tones; can't hear spoken output from a computer.
Approach
- Use visual redundancy (e.g., See Beep—currently in public domain— flashes the screen each time the computer beeps).

Barrier   Individual can't hear disk drives and cannot tell when they are in operation if no visual indicator is provided.
Approach
- Use Norton Utilities (on Macintosh) to show the menu bar icon when disk drives are working.

Compensatory Strategies for Individuals with Hearing Impairments

People who are hearing impaired or deaf can use adaptive devices to communicate with other individuals and to enhance their efforts in completing class assignments.

Difficulty   Individual has trouble taking notes in class (trying to watch an interpreter sign a lecture or read a professor's lips and writing notes at the same time).
Strategies
- Use a laptop computer to take notes (in addition to an interpreter who signs the professor's lecture). This allows the individual to watch the interpreter and touch type, rather than trying to watch the interpreter and write at the same time.)
- Use specialized stenographic-type key entry (e.g., RapidText) that can provide closed-captioned information and a printout of the entire lecture. (A person must be specially trained on this equipment.)

Difficulty   Individual has difficulty accessing university administrative services (e.g., registration by phone or information services).

Strategies
- Use online registration materials.
- Make TTYs or TDDs available in administrative offices.

LEARNING DISABILITIES

Individuals who have learning disabilities generally have little difficulty gaining access to computer hardware and software. For the most part, their access problems are really how to most effectively use computer hardware and software, what teaching strategies facilitate learning, and how to use a computer.

However, some individuals with learning disabilities do have particular problems accessing computers. For example, individuals who have visual processing problems due to a learning disability may encounter the same barriers as individuals who have low vision. In those cases, individuals with learning disabilities should try the same approaches as listed under barriers to computer access by individuals with low vision.

People with learning disabilities may also have motor problems and problems processing oral instructions and conversations. For these individuals, see the section on mobility impairment strategies and approaches and also see the section on hearing impairment approaches and strategies.

Computer Access Approaches for Individuals with Learning Disabilities

Some people with learning disabilities may need special attention during their computer training. They may need more time, more review, or a quieter environment than other individuals.

Barrier   Individual has difficulty finding place on screen.
Approaches (see also approaches for people with vision impairments)
- Use an enlarged cursor.
- Show only one line or word of print on screen at a time.
- Experiment with various type sizes and fonts.
- Experiment with margin and line widths.
- Experiment with pixel density (e.g., VGA display with solid letters might be easier to perceive than broken-up CGA letters).
- Highlight portions of text.
- Use magnification hardware or software.
- Use a screen-reading program with speech synthesis.

Compensatory Strategies for Individuals with Learning Disabilities

Individuals with learning disabilities can compete successfully with their peers by using adapted computers and various kinds of software to compensate for various difficulties related to their learning disabilities.

Difficulty Individual has trouble visually tracking copy on the printed page.
Strategies
- Use a copy holder with line guides.
- Display one line of text on a CCTV.

Difficulty Individual has problems spelling.
Strategies
- Use computer software that checks spelling.
- Use online dictionaries and thesauruses.
- Use abbreviation expansion software.
- Use word-prediction software.
- Use a voice recognition system.

Difficulty Individual has problems organizing ideas and information.
Strategies
- Use outlining software (e.g., Microsoft Word outline feature and GrandView Think Tank). Note, however, that these programs provide some support for individuals with learning disabilities, but they're useless unless the individual knows how to outline. They should initially be used with a tutor who can give individuals assistance in learning outlining skills.
- Use a word processor with word expansion and abbreviation, a spelling checker, and thesaurus features.
- Use online calendars and planners.

Difficulty Individual has problems with writing mechanics, language structure, and vocabulary.
Strategies
- Use online grammar manuals, dictionaries, thesauruses, word usage checkers, and structural analyses.
- Use a screen-reading program with a speech synthesizer.
- Use a voice recognition system.

Difficulty Individual has difficulty translating thought into written format, but the individual has good oral language ability.
Strategy
- Use a voice recognition system.

Difficulty   Individual has problems proofreading written tests and assignments.
Strategies
- Use a voice synthesis system (e.g., screen-reading software with speech synthesizer or Sound-Proof) to take tests and to produce assignments.
- Use online structural analyses.
- Use software that checks word usage.
- Use grammar checking software.

SPEECH IMPAIRMENTS

The biggest benefit of adaptive computer technology for people with speech impairments comes from compensatory strategies. Traditional computers with keyboards and screens pose no access barriers for a person who has a speech impairment, assuming that the individual has no other disabilities. However, many people with speech impairments do have other disability-related problems. For example, an individual with cerebral palsy might have both speech and hand coordination difficulties. In that case, the approaches for overcoming computer access barriers can be found in the discussion of mobility impairment strategies.

Compensatory Strategies for Individuals with Speech Impairments

Individuals who have difficulty speaking can use adaptive devices to communicate with other individuals and to participate in the classroom environment.

Difficulty   Individual has problems asking questions in class, communicating with campus personnel, and communicating with classmates during group discussions.
Strategies
- Use a laptop computer with augmentative communication software.
- Use specialized augmentative communication system that has speech output, visual display, and printed output capabilities.
- Use a TDD for phone information and communication.

Difficulty   Individual has problems communicating in a timely manner with augmentative communication device.
Strategy
- Use rate enhancement strategies such as abbreviation expansion, word prediction, and semantic compaction (i.e., icons used to encode messages).

TRAUMATIC BRAIN INJURY

Devising an adaptive computer system to help compensate for the difficulties that a person with traumatic brain injury or multiple disabilities experiences usually means combining several adaptive techniques. This is because people who have traumatic brain injury often have a combination of disabilities, each of which might require different compensatory strategies.

When devising a computer system that provides access and compensatory strategies for people with traumatic brain injury, a good starting place is to look at the difficulties and recommended procedures for people with similar disabilities. For example, people with posttraumatic brain damage may have no use of their hands. In such cases, the access approaches and compensatory strategies might be the same as those listed for people with physical impairments. People with traumatic brain injury might have vision problems, in which case the approaches and strategies recommended for people who have low vision or who are blind might help.

People with traumatic brain damage may also have some of the difficulties that people with learning disabilities have. These include short- or long-term memory impairment, perceptual difficulties, and language impairments, which in an academic setting might be manifested as difficulties in reading, writing, researching, and organizing information.

These impairments will definitely limit how effectively a student learns in school, and may also limit the complexity of the adaptive computer devices the individual is able to use. In cases where the individual is recovering from a traumatic brain injury, be sure to consult with other professionals who are assisting in the individual's rehabilitation. Be aware that some compensatory or access strategies may be counterproductive to the recovery process. For example, the use of a reading machine by an individual regaining cognitive abilities after coming out of a coma may assist—or impede—the individual's success in regaining reading abilities.

Compensatory Strategies for Individuals with Brain Injury

Difficulty   Individual has problems remembering daily schedule.
Strategies
- Use electronic organizers (a wide range are available in office supply stores).
- Use watches with timers.
- Use computer calendars.

GENERAL STRATEGIES AND APPROACHES
FOR ALL DISABILITY TYPES

A good deal of the time, approaches to access barriers and compensatory strategies don't need to be complicated or expensive. Sometimes a little common sense goes a very long way. For example, a strategically placed lamp, enlarged screen print, or Braille labels placed over certain keys on the keyboard will help individuals with some types of vision impairments.

Many individuals have already developed strategies to meet some or all of their needs, and they're probably willing to share their ideas. Be sure to make use of their experience. For example, although no single solution will accommodate all people with learning disabilities, discussions with and among individuals with such disabilities may lead to approaches that can be used to help others.

It is important to make adaptive computer systems adjustable to other systems and equipment. If possible, the adaptive systems shouldn't interfere with the computer's usual use. Incorporate tables and chairs with adjustable heights, hardware that increases the volume of auditory output, and alternative keyboards so they can be used with standard hardware. Adjustability is important to accommodate the variations in the type and extent of disabilities among individuals and to accommodate individual users with progressive conditions such as muscular dystrophy or diabetes. Generally, the adaptation criteria for computers should permit the greatest access to computers. That can be accomplished by making sure that the adaptive devices function well with standard computing software such as WordPerfect and Microsoft Word, and standard databases and spreadsheets. The adaptive devices should be compatible with other adaptive equipment that is in general use, and they should function with the standard computing hardware in use on campus.

It is best to make use of adaptive technology and equipment that has a short learning and training time. In some cases, there's no choice but to go with a complicated package, but make reasonable learning time a primary goal. Also be prepared to have staff members available to help individuals use the adaptive equipment.

Try to be practical as your school purchases adaptive hardware and software. Equipment packages that can be used by multiple individuals and packages that have a reasonable purchase price are preferable to the more expensive packages that may not provide any additional capability.

IMPORTANT REMINDERS

As much as possible, solicit information from other experts in this field:

- Occupational, physical, and speech therapists.

- Vendors (about pricing and loans, product trials, and return provisions).
- Other schools in your area, with whom it may be possible to work out a loan or exchange of adaptive equipment.
- Disability organizations.
- Local businesses that have hired disabled people.
- Tech Act offices.

CHAPTER

Issues in Science, Engineering, and Mathematics

Raman, currently a computer scientist at Adobe Systems, Inc., is blind. He went through school, including college in India, before doing his graduate work at Cornell University in New York. To get through his curriculum—which included a large component of mathematics and science classes—Raman used a Braille slate to take notes. In India, Raman employed readers to record books, which he would then paraphrase in Braille notes. In the United States, Raman made use of organizations such as Recording for the Blind and Dyslexic to make tapes, but he still continued to prepare his own Braille notes based on the tapes. The advantage of the Braille notes was that rather than having to listen to a full six-hour tape, he could skim through his notes at a leisurely pace.

Here are few tips on using taped versions of texts:

- Students should make use of the advantages provided by computer technology.
- Students should not give up on a course or program of study simply because the required texts are not on tape.
- If students can't find a tape for the particular recommended edition of a textbook, they should look for a previous edition or a similar text by a different author. Students should use what is available on tape and supplement that, using readers who read from the class text what is missing from the other volume.

Raman recommends TeX/LaTeX for writing mathematics. The advantage is that it is a fairly simple notation at first (which gets more difficult as the math gets more difficult), and at the end of the day, students will be able to produce clear and reliable output for instructors to review. Raman urges students to produce output that instructors can work with, rather than hope that instructors will be lenient in what they require from disabled students. That leniency can unintentionally prevent a student from getting the most out of a class. Raman is a firm believer that students should take responsibility for their own educations, and that getting professors, school administrators, or employers to make accommodations for individuals with disabilities will only happen when individuals become self-advocates.

The bottom line, he says, is that the more disabled students make their presence felt in class and the more actively they participate in class, the less likely it is that they'll be passed by. (This is, of course, true for any student.) The two most important things for disabled students to do, he says, are to sit in the front of the class so the instructor doesn't forget their presence and to insist (gently) that instructors verbalize everything that they write on blackboards.

ACCESS TO SCIENCE, ENGINEERING, AND MATHEMATICS

Most people who have been through high school have at one time or another struggled with a mathematical equation or scratched their heads trying to figure out exactly what a molecular structure is supposed to look like. Imagine trying to do those equations or understand those molecular structures if you couldn't see them. Imagine trying to operate a Bunsen burner if you couldn't use your hands. Although science, engineering, and mathematics are difficult for many people, they can be even more difficult for people with disabilities.

And because there are difficulties in both learning and teaching science, engineering, and mathematics to students with disabilities, it has not been uncommon for schools, colleges, and universities to shut disabled students out of classes in those fields. When they're denied access to science and math classes, though, students with disabilities are denied a full liberal arts education because most colleges and universities have core course requirements in science and mathematics that apply to all undergraduates. In the past, students with disabilities were sometimes excused from taking certain courses or were held to lower academic standards, but this policy is not wise or necessary. Today, students with disabilities can—and should—study science and mathematics alongside their peers.

Technology is beginning to make the difficulties that people with disabilities face when they study or work in the fields of science and technology a little easier. And that's good news, both for people with disabilities and for the rest of the country. Businesses report the need to hire people who are trained in the same fields in which people with disabilities have long been underrepresented, and with new and developing computer technology, more disabled people can study, conduct research, and work in the fields of science, engineering, and mathematics.

There are three main barriers that have historically limited disabled people from studying and working in technical fields. First, individuals with disabilities have traditionally faced negative attitudes—both in education and in the workplace—about their capabilities in these fields. Second, individuals with disabilities face obstacles because of inaccessible buildings, computers, and laboratories. And finally, individuals with disabilities often have difficulty completing certain tasks, such as accessing and producing mathematical equations and scientific notation.

NEGATIVE ATTITUDES AND PERCEPTIONS

A 1989 study by the National Science Foundation (*Changing America*) reported that negative attitudes on the part of faculty and employers constitute the single most significant barrier faced by disabled individuals. Students with disabilities often face negative attitudes about their abilities from administrators, faculty members, and even their own parents. This is particularly harmful because not only does it deny or limit some students' entrance into the fields of science, engineering, and math, but it almost ensures that those individuals will never be able to enter careers in those disciplines when they enter the workforce.

It's not right that a student should be barred from these fields simply because he or she is in a wheelchair and can't pull up to a computer in a school lab because the table isn't adjustable. Unfortunately, many schools across the United States are still making excuses—and exceptions—for disabled students. When a school tells an eighth grader that because his wheelchair doesn't fit in the computer lab, he can spend his computer time doing some other activity, that school is denying him the right to learn about computers, and it may be denying society a gifted engineer.

Unfortunately, disabled students are often quietly discouraged from certain fields, and they conclude that their teachers and others view them negatively. This problem is compounded by the lack of resources to assist students with disabilities. As a result, faculty may not understand how to accommodate students with special needs; classrooms, laboratories, and whole programs may not be modified to provide appropriate access. As students miss the chance to study these fields in elementary and secondary school, they find themselves unable to compete in collegiate level science, engineering, and math. Consequently, colleges and universities rarely make special efforts to recruit students with disabilities into these fields. New Mexico State University, Northeastern University, the University of Washington, and the University of California at Los Angeles have developed special outreach programs to recruit disabled students into electronics, engineering, mathematics, and science, but few collegiate programs for underrepresented students include people with disabilities.

According to recent studies and conference reports from the American Association for the Advancement of Science, some college administrators and faculty do not believe that students with disabilities can perform well in science, engineering, and mathematics. That simply is not true. What is true is that students with disabilities need alternative ways to access information in order to study and learn. If students with disabilities are going to be given the same opportunities as everyone else to study and work in these fields, and if the United States is to benefit from the technical acumen of individuals who happen to be disabled, then negative perceptions must be eased and colleges and universities must willingly provide opportunities.

Although there are more than 100,000 employed scientists and engineers with disabilities, few colleges and universities are explicitly providing disabled students with the tools that can help them enter these fields after their formal education is completed. There are many effective transition programs around the country for women and minorities to help bridge the gap to college programs and the workplace, but far too few transition programs are devoted to students with disabilities. Unfortunately, even individuals with disabilities who have managed to gain a proper background and expertise in these fields are often denied jobs in their chosen fields because employers doubt their ability to perform the necessary work.

INACCESSIBLE BUILDINGS, COMPUTERS, AND LABORATORIES

Even as the Rehabilitation Act of 1968 and the more recent Americans with Disabilities Act have mandated accessible buildings, the physical accessibility of math and science buildings, and the computing laboratories themselves, may be inadequate. In those labs, individuals may have problems using equipment or safely maneuvering throughout the facility. They may not be able to use standard laboratory instruments such as Bunsen burners, microscopes, and calculators. See Chapter 5 for more information on accessible laboratories and facilities.

There also may be compatibility problems in accessing computer operating systems with adaptive computer software. In science, engineering, and mathematics, major operating systems include DOS, OS/2, Windows, UNIX, and Macintosh. Access to these diverse systems with adaptive computing technologies is varied and sometimes problematic. Voice synthesis access is well established in DOS; access to UNIX and X-Windows is still in development.

As a basic foundation for access to science, engineering, and mathematics, look at the general adaptive computing solutions. Individuals who are working

and studying in the technical fields will undoubtedly need the basic accommodations discussed in Chapters 7 and 8 as a foundation for the more sophisticated strategies that are discussed here.

Laboratory Adaptations

Creating a laboratory for people with disabilities poses several requirements.
For people with vision impairments, it is necessary to modify the laboratory
equipment so that students and researchers can manipulate instruments and
read data. For people with mobility impairments, it is necessary to arrange labs
so that people with wheelchairs, scooters, and crutches can maneuver safely
and can operate equipment. It is also important to configure and label every
piece of equipment so that people with disabilities can identify all aspects of
the laboratory.

Physical accessibility for a scientific laboratory can be achieved through the
use of wide aisles, adjustable-height tables, adjustable keyboards and monitors,
easy-to-reach power strips and lighting, and lab documentation that is available in alternate formats. In addition to physical access to the laboratory,
students with disabilities may need adaptations to provide access to instruments and apparatus. The best source of information for simple accommodations is the handbook "Teaching Chemistry to Students with Disabilities,"
published by the American Chemical Society. Although the primary audience
for this handbook is chemistry teachers, it is useful in any scientific or
technical discipline. An electronic version is available on the EASI web page
at http://www.rit.edu/~easi/easisem/chem.html.

The introduction of microcomputer-based experiments into instructional
science labs now makes it possible for students with a variety of disabilities to
do "hands-on, minds-on" science. Any student who can see the computer can
use combinations of off-the-shelf products to perform a microcomputer-based
experiment. This opens an opportunity to include disabled students in the
mainstream of science education in ways that they have rarely been included
before. The students who can't use off-the-shelf hardware and software are
those who can't see the computer screen. That is because commercial software
for computer-aided experimentation is almost entirely graphics based. Some
students with low vision can use screen magnification software, but for
students who are blind, there is nothing commercially available. Researchers
at East Carolina University (ECU), in Greenville, North Carolina, are currently trying to ameliorate that problem by developing software that will allow
blind students to acquire and analyze laboratory data using synthetic speech,
tones, electronic music, enlarged graphs, and very large text. The software
runs on widely available, relatively inexpensive hardware.

The ECU group has designed a talking, whistling, large-text laboratory
workstation that consists of an IBM-compatible PC and the Team Labs

Personal Science Laboratory (PSL, formerly made by IBM) with probes, an electronic balance, and a digital multimeter (DMM) equipped with a serial port. The workstation software runs under DOS and uses the Creative Labs Sound Blaster sound card for output of speech, music, and other sounds. With this workstation, a blind student will be able to make independent measurements of mass, temperature, pH, light intensity, AC and DC voltages and currents, resistance, frequency, and capacitance. The group also plans to write software to read ultraviolet-visible and infrared spectrophotometers.

The workstation software gives spoken readings through the Sound Blaster (or other speech synthesizer) and displays the readings in very large text on the screen. In most of the programs, readings can be taken manually or automatically at fixed time intervals and can also be stored in a disk file for later analysis. The system thus functions as an automatic data logger and as an electronic laboratory notebook.

The DMM program has several unusual features. It announces the meter's ranges as they are changed and also tells the user if there is an overflow. If the meter is in a hazardous range, the Sound Blaster makes obnoxious noises and gives the user a spoken warning. The workstation software is not yet complete, but it will be made available as freeware as soon as it is finished. The first part of the software to be released will be a program that reads the output of Ohaus electronic balances through a serial port and presents mass readings and instructions for the user as speech and as very large text on the computer screen.

The talking balance program should be helpful to students with limited manual dexterity as well as to vision-impaired students. After the balance is turned on, there are no more buttons to push. The large visual display will also be easy to read from a wheelchair. (The displays on many electronic balances are difficult to read from a seated position, especially if the balance is on a high lab bench.)

Most "personal data assistants" for blind people have serial ports and can be programmed to send commands to an external instrument and read its serial output. The readings can be converted to speech or, on some devices, displayed in tactile form such as Braille characters on an electromechanical Braille display. The most popular personal data assistant of this sort is probably the Braille'n'Speak (BNS), manufactured by Blazie Engineering. The BNS is a small, portable device that has seven keys for input of Braille, 640K of memory, a serial port, and synthetic speech output.

The use of BNS to read instruments with serial ports has two important advantages over using an adapted computer. The first is cost. Often, a blind science student will already own a BNS or similar device. Second, the learning curve is not steep either for the student or for the teacher. Personal data assistants are also available from many other manufacturers. The primary requirement for their use in reading digital instruments is the presence of a programmable bi-directional serial port.

Laser Stereolithography

Laser stereolithography, a process that produces three-dimensional plastic models from images created in computer-aided design (CAD) programs, has been used to fabricate tactile molecular models that can be used by blind and visually impaired individuals. Size, shape, and surface texture of the models allow a person to distinguish various types of atoms. Three-dimensional stereolithographic models can also be made to represent concepts and spatial relationships other than atoms. These models will allow blind and visually-impaired individuals to get a full understanding of concepts that are critical in many areas of chemistry, physics, biology, and mathematics. For more information, see Skawinski, Busanic, Ofsievich, Luhkov, and Venanzi, "The Use of Laser Stereolithography." Articles in *Information Technology and Disabilities* are archived on the St. John's University gopher. To access the journal via gopher, locate the St. John's University (New York) gopher. Select "Disability and Rehabilitation Resources," and from the next menu, select "EASI: Equal Access to Software and Information." *Information Technology and Disabilities* is an item on the EASI menu.

ACCESSING AND PRODUCING EQUATIONS AND NOTATIONS

Many people with disabilities, especially those with vision or physical impairments, rely on the provision of, and access to, electronic text to do their work. People with vision impairments, if they have electronic versions of texts, can convert material to Braille, or they can have it read aloud using a computer, speech synthesizer, and software. Individuals with physical impairments that limit their hand movement can use adapted computers to produce written information.

While electronic ASCII files provide access to many materials, there are serious problems in science, mathematics, and engineering because certain necessary symbols are not part of the traditional ASCII character set. Moreover, the printed page of mathematical equations does not readily allow translation by scanning/optical character recognition systems into a symbol-by-symbol, line-by-line ASCII document. Consequently, it is not possible to scan and translate directly from a typical mathematics equation or scientific formula to an ASCII equivalent. Braille presents similar problems. Because Braille was created to help blind people read the Bible, mathematical and scientific notation were never considered.

Many science, engineering, and mathematics texts present information that is expressed graphically. For students who are blind or have impaired vision, converting graphs into raised line drawings can provide access. However, people are generally unable to perceive as much detail from raised line drawings as they do from visual images. Vision impairments may also be associated with reduced tactile responses, such as in the case of partial blindness caused by diabetes. Braille-raised graphics also have a low resolution value, which makes detailed representation difficult. In addition, the process for integrating texts and graphics in tactile form on a page—critical for science texts—is currently not widely implemented in most science texts.

Nemeth Code and Mathematical/Symbolic Braille

Most individuals with vision impairments use either Braille or electronic versions of text to access written material. However, special problems exist in working with mathematical equations in Braille because traditional Braille does not include mathematical symbols and most symbols used in higher mathematics are not part of the traditional ASCII character set. This makes it impossible to scan printed mathematical equations into an electronic format. In 1965, Professor Abraham Nemeth of the University of Detroit addressed this problem by publishing a method for writing mathematical equations in Braille.

Before printing, many documents in "literal" Braille are converted to Grade II Braille. Grade II Braille uses contractions and concatenations that greatly reduce the size of a finished document. If a mathematical equation in literal Braille is converted into Grade II Braille, there is a high possibility that the translation software will automatically contract and concatenate the equation, making it unreadable or misleading. Another possibility is that the translator may replace a mathematical symbol with a word description or instruction. For example, $1 + 2 = 3$ may be translated into *1 plus 2 equals 3.* That may be acceptable in some cases, but not in others.

To prevent these translations from occurring, it is necessary that the Braille translation software drop out of Grade II Braille when a mathematical equation appears and begin using literal Braille, which is a character translation. Then the Nemeth Code, which substitutes usable ASCII symbols to represent the mathematical symbols, can be used. Creating mathematical notation with Nemeth Code requires a software package that converts ASCII files to Grade II Braille and control codes that instruct the software translation package to drop out of Grade II Braille and go to literal Braille for equations. The Nemeth Code symbols are then inserted in literal Braille. While this system has been beneficial, it is time consuming and expensive.

Arizona State University has been using the Nemeth Code and Duxbury Braille Translation software to efficiently create readable mathematical/symbolic Braille. For more information on using the Nemeth Code to produce mathematical equations, see Flechsig and Jones, "Converting Text to Braille."

Raised Line Drawings

Sometimes raised line drawings are the best way to reproduce graphic information so that people with vision impairments can use it. This can be a relatively easy task that requires a software "paint" package, such as PC PaintBrush and a software "capture" package that coverts images into embossable ASCII format. VersaPoint Graphics from TeleSensory is one package that performs this function well.

Creating usable raised line drawings depends on the proper use of textures, pixel density, definite boundaries, and clear labels. It is also important to remember that although raised line drawings can be helpful for individuals with visual impairments, tactile images cannot represent as much detail as visual images. For more information, see Jones, "Converting Graphical Information."

AsTeR: Audio System for Technical Readings

Electronic documents make it possible to have information available in more than the traditional visual form. Electronic information can now be display-independent. The Audio System for Technical Readings (AsTeR) is a computing system that formats electronic documents to produce audio documents in a manner that allows the listener to either read an entire document or browse the internal structure of a document and read only selected portions. AsTeR can speak literary texts as well as highly technical documents that contain complex mathematics.

Visual communication is characterized by the eye's ability to actively access parts of a two-dimensional display. The reader is active, and the display is passive. This active-passive role is reversed during aural communication, where information flows to a passive listener. This reversed relationship prevents a person from having multiple views of the information and makes it more difficult to understand complex material. It is not possible for a listener to get an overall view of the information and then zoom in on the details. This shortcoming of audio information becomes more problematic when the information being presented is complex mathematics. Audio formatting, which uses various tones and pitches to produce an auditory display, overcomes these problems. AsTeR is an interactive system that allows listeners to browse the information structure of a document, as well as the information being presented.

TeX is a typesetting system widely used in the mathematics and science communities to typeset technical documents from journal articles to textbooks. A TeX file is an ASCII file with embedded TeX commands to indicate mathematical symbols; for example, \alpha for the first letter of the Greek alphabet. AsTeR produces audio-formatted documents from the electronic source of the TeX documents. AsTeR works with most of the popular dialects of TeX. The combination of LaTeX and AsTeR makes it possible to use a command set that expresses the semantic content of a symbol, as well as its typographical form.

TeX makes it possible to write documents that express both the typographical and semantic content of mathematical symbols. The typographical features enable TeX to produce high-quality typeset output. The semantic content enables AsTeR to produce high-quality aural renderings.

AsTeR has parsing and expressive capabilities that auditorially present the structure and content of a mathematical formula in ways similar to graphical displays. AsTeR also has hypertext facilities that allow a random search for information.

AsTeR is not currently available for general use, although it has seen rapid developments in the past year. For an interactive demonstration of AsTeR on the World Wide Web, go to: http://www.cs.cornell.edu/Info/People/raman/aster/aster-toplevel.html. An AsTeR-generated, recorded version of this thesis is available from Recording for the Blind and Dyslexic as Order No. FB190 (for more information, see Raman, "AsTeR").

TRIANGLE

TRIANGLE is a utility program that provides Braille access to UNIX applications that can be run in text mode. It runs under the DOS operating system and is as trimodal (accessible visually, orally, or through Braille) as possible within present technology. It is intended to be a tool for reading, writing, and manipulating information, including mathematical equations, complicated tables, and various kinds of graphs, diagrams, and tables.

A graphing calculator is part of TRIANGLE, and its output can be "viewed" on the computer screen. It can also be heard as a tone graph or felt by a moving Braille icon as the x-coordinate is varied. The graph may also be printed on a Braille printer. Flow diagrams, computer tree diagrams, and a number of other types of information typically presented graphically for sighted readers have been translated into "Braille diagrams" that blind students have found fairly understandable. Some of the simpler diagrams of this kind can often be read using a refreshable Braille display, even though these displays show only one line at a time. TRIANGLE provides a Braille reader for such Braille diagrams.

Many such diagrams and most other graphical information are more easily understood if available as a tactile picture that can be viewed on a digitizing pad so that the computer can supply additional information. TRIANGLE includes this capability.

A number of translator programs will be made available in order to make TRIANGLE as useful as possible. At a minimum, these will include programs to translate LaTeX, MS Word, and WordPerfect files into the GS notation used by TRIANGLE, translation of standard spreadsheet files to the GS table form, and translation of the computer map files generated for figures by the Nomad and AudioPIX software. (GS notation is a compact linear representation for math, equivalent to that used in the TeX languages.) For more information on TRIANGLE, see: http://dots.physics.orst.edu.

Dotsplus

Dotsplus is a method for producing hard copy scientific literature that is usable by people with visual impairments and people with vision-related learning disabilities. The layout of a Dotsplus document closely resembles its corresponding print document. Dotsplus symbols are larger by a factor of approximately 2.5, but most of the mathematical and scientific symbols (plus, minus, equals, parentheses, brackets, integral sign, etc.) are raised images that look like their print equivalents. Some are emphasized to make tactile recognition easier, but all are instantly recognizable by sighted readers. Letters, numbers, and a few symbols that are difficult to recognize tactually are reproduced in an eight-dot Braille code. Symbol position is the same as it would be in an ink-print version of the document. In Dotsplus, Braille code must be one in which the cell shape, without reference to its position, is sufficient for symbol identification. The lower case Dotsplus letters are standard Braille.

Dotsplus documents can be printed from LaTeX files and from some graphics-based word processor files. Original files may be viewed and edited on a graphics screen or printed for sighted viewers.

Dotsplus documents can be printed with the use of a modified wax-jet printer that produces tactile images, or they can be printed on special "swell" paper using most standard printers. The swell paper is then fed through a machine that heats the paper, causing the black portions to swell.

For more information on Dotsplus, see Barry, Gardner, and Lundquist, "Books for Blind Scientists."

NOMAD Pad

The NOMAD pad is a "talking," touch-sensitive pad on which raised-line graphics are placed. It is connected to a personal computer, into which files describing graphics have been loaded. When the appropriate file is selected, the user can touch various points on the graphic, and NOMAD will describe the graphics though synthetic speech. The NOMAD pad is particularly useful describing geography, geometry, biology, physics, astronomy, and other fields that make heavy use of charts, graphs, diagrams, and spatial concepts. The pad is 22-3/8 inches by 15-3/8 inches and weighs about 6-1/2 pounds. It has an internal speech synthesizer that has both English and Spanish capabilities. The pad runs on electricity or battery. NOMAD can be connected to any IBM-compatible or Macintosh computer, although a special kit is required for Macintosh use.

RESOURCE ORGANIZATIONS

This list includes some of the many organizations that are working to promote access to science, engineering, and mathematics. These organizations are a good place to start compiling information about this area of access.

American Association for the Advancement of Science
1333 H Street, NW
Washington, DC 20005
Voice/TTY: 202-326-6649
Internet: info@aaas.org

DO-IT (Disabilities, Opportunity, Internetworking & Technology)
University of Washington
Computing & Communications
Mail Stop JE-25
Seattle, WA 98195
Voice/TTY: 206-685-DOIT
Internet: doit@u.washington.edu

EASI (Equal Access to Software and Information)
P.O. Box 18928
Rochester, NY 14618
Phone: 716-244-9065
Fax: 716-475-7120
E-mail: easi@educom.edu
Web: http://www.rit.edu/~easi

Foundation for Science and Disabilities
236 Grant St.
Morgantown, WV 26505-7509
Phone: 304-293-6363

HEATH Resource Center
One Dupont Cir., Ste 800
Washington, DC 20036
Voice/TTY: 202-939-9320
Internet: heath@ace.nche.edu

National Science Foundation
4201 Wilson Blvd.
Arlington, VA 22230
Phone: 703-306-1636
Internet: info@nsf.gov
Web: http://www.nsf.gov

Recording for the Blind and Dyslexic
20 Roszel Rd.
Princeton, NJ 08540
Phone: 609-452-0606 or 800-221-4792
Internet: info@rfbd.org

TRACE Research and Development Center
S-151 Waisman Center
1500 Highland Ave.
Madison, WI 53705
Phone: 608-262-6966
TDD: 608-262-5408
Internet: essers@macc.wisc.edu

MODEL PROJECTS

Several organizations are working on specific projects to increase the number
of individuals with disabilities working in the fields of science, engineering,
and mathematics. Below are descriptions of a project that prepares high school
students for postsecondary education and a project that focuses on making
college and university science, engineering, and mathematics programs accessible.

DO-IT
(Disabilities, Opportunity, Internetworking & Technology)

The University of Washington is working on a project to increase the participation of disabled individuals in science, engineering and mathematics programs and careers. DO-IT began in 1992 and is primarily funded by the
National Science Foundation.

The DO-IT Scholars program provides opportunities for high school students in their sophomore or junior years to study science, engineering, and
mathematics through an innovative program that combines a mentor program, online interaction, and a short stint living on a university campus. The
program is aimed at developing self-advocacy skills and using technology to
pursue academic interests.

DO-IT scholars use computers and the Internet to explore academic and career interests. They are introduced to adaptive technologies, establish local Internet connections, and receive in-home training. Industry mentors work with scholars through electronic communications and personal meetings, and there is a summer study program in which scholars live in dorms at the University of Washington, both to get a feel of campus life and to participate in lectures and labs that use computers and the Internet. Subjects include oceanography; heart surgery; chemistry; virtual reality; geophysics; material sciences; civil, mechanical, and electrical engineering; mathematics; biology; physics; and astronomy. For more information on this program, contact DO-IT (contact information in previous section).

EASI (Equal Access to Software and Information)

EASI, an organization affiliated with the American Association for Higher Education, developed a compendium of information on math and science access during a two-year grant for the National Science Foundation. The goal of the project was to take information that tells how to make science, engineering, and mathematics materials accessible to people with disabilities and distribute that information to the people who need it. The materials are directed at faculty who teach science, engineering, and mathematics; school administrators; and researchers and students with disabilities.

EASI has a five-pronged dissemination plan to make sure that all materials for this project are accessible and available to the people who need them:

- Project representatives make presentations at disability and disciplinary conferences.
- Project representatives are teaching interactive online courses on science, engineering, and mathematics access.
- A series of three videos called "EASI Street to Science, Engineering and Mathematics" is available.
- A series of publications has been created, printed, and distributed.
- The Internet is being used to post and distribute all publications and materials that are created through this project.

EASI has recently begun work on a second NSF grant. This grant project will focus on science and math access for K–12 students with disabilities. For more information on these projects, contact EASI (contact information in previous section).

CHAPTER 10

Creating Accessible Libraries

N orm Coombs had written and published a textbook long before he
ever had the chance to look at it himself. It was the early 1970s, and
Norm, who is blind and who didn't know how to use a computer at
that time, typed the book on a regular typewriter. Editing the book required
extensive help from a reader, and by the time the book was in print, it no
longer resembled the Braille copy that he had kept for himself. Because Norm
had no way to access a library catalog back then, he just had to take other
people's word for it that the book actually was in the catalog and that he was
listed as the author. It wasn't until almost 10 years later that Norm first started
using a computer with speech output. Coincidentally, his college put its library
catalog online at the same time. Using his own computer and speech synthesizer, one of the first citations that Norm looked up was his own book. It was
there, right where it belonged, with Norman Coombs, Ph.D., listed as the
author.

ACCESS TO THE KNOWLEDGE OF THE WORLD

Take the knowledge of the world, encode it as ink on paper, bind it, classify it,
catalog it, put it inside a building, store it on shelves, and then lock the doors
and don't let anyone inside. That, in effect, is historically what has been done
to people with disabilities.

Most able-bodied people take the library for granted. For children, getting
a first library card is a rite of passage. It opens up a world of ideas and fantasy
to them. From the age of five years, most people are able to browse the stacks,
picking and choosing from among the many volumes, dipping into whatever

subject or story strikes their fancies. Later, when they're older, they use the library to study for exams, and they research the information needed for their papers and projects—and for their lives. For many people, even after they're grown, the library remains an important resource for enjoyment and continuing education.

But for many people with disabilities, the library—and the knowledge it contains—has been forbidden territory. There were public libraries that people couldn't enter because they couldn't walk up steps. And some people who could gain access to the building were unable to access the knowledge contained in an ink-on-paper format because of what we call "print handicaps"—the inability to use materials printed on paper. Some people have print handicaps due to blindness or vision impairments. Some have mobility impairments that limit their ability to hold a book or paper. And some have learning disabilities that limit their ability to process printed material. In the past, people with these disabilities have been limited in their use of libraries.

But now all that is changing. The rapid development of adaptive computing technology and electronic information challenges librarians to provide services to all people. Electronic documents and databases, coupled with adaptive computer technology, permit people with print handicaps to be included within the population of library users. The challenge for libraries and librarians is how to provide information and services to this group of new users.

Attempts to provide access to written knowledge for people with print handicaps began about a century ago with scattered programs offered by big-city libraries. Then, libraries scheduled special readings of books for blind people and others as part of its service to the community. Or a library included a few embossed editions of books in its collection. Later, specialized organizations, such as the National Library Service and Recording for the Blind and Dyslexic, developed books in alternative formats—either tactile print or audio recordings—and made them available to people with vision impairments. In addition, some religious organizations loaned out religion books in Braille and on tape. It has only been during the past 20 years or so, however, that there has been a move to make all libraries accessible to all people, including those with disabilities. There are two main reasons for this—computers and politics.

Computers have changed the way the world does business, and libraries are no exception. Libraries are using computers to catalog and store much of their information. At the same time, people with disabilities are using adaptive technology to gain access to the world of computers and the benefits of that technology. Catalogs, journals, and other reference materials that were once available only through the services of a reader, as an audio recording, or a Braille translation, suddenly became available by computer. This helped feed the growing political movement of people with disabilities demanding equal access to the mainstream of society.

PROVIDING ACCESSIBLE TERMINALS IN LIBRARIES

There are certain standards that must be met by all libraries, whether public or in schools. One or more of the computer terminals available to library users must include the adaptive software and hardware necessary to serve patrons with disabilities. The accessible computers should be on adjustable-height tables to accommodate wheelchairs. Since many people in wheelchairs do not need adaptive software, it is a good idea to put all computers on adjustable tables if possible. That opens all the computers to people in wheelchairs and frees up the adaptive computer stations for those who need it. Many people will be using the computers, so the library staff needs to make sure that workstations are kept free of stray books and papers, that the cables are neatly stowed out of the way, and that access to computers is not blocked by chairs or other obstacles.

If Braille overlays have been installed on the computer keyboards, the staff needs to check them periodically to make sure they have not fallen off or moved around on the keys. If a screen reader or voice input device is available at the adaptive terminal, steps should be taken to isolate that station so as not to disturb other library patrons.

OTHER PROVISIONS FOR PATRONS WITH DISABILITIES

The modern library is more than just books. It also has audiotapes and videotapes containing a wide range of information. It is the library's responsibility to make these materials accessible. Library videos should be closed-captioned for patrons with hearing disabilities. Audio materials should also be available in a printed format. Some videos have a feature that provides a narrative of what is happening for people with vision impairments. The library should also have a telephone with TTY capabilities so deaf patrons can call in for information. A public phone for patrons should also be equipped with such capability.

ACCESS TO ELECTRONIC INFORMATION IN THE LIBRARY

In the past decade, all library patrons have benefited from the amount of information that is available online. Chapter 11 will go into great detail about the power and possibilities that exist for people with disabilities who have access to the Internet—there's a wealth of information, exciting and mundane, that can be accessed from a desktop computer by an individual sitting in a home, school, or office. People with access to the Internet can do everything from communicating with others who share the same passions to conducting research for a doctoral thesis.

Information is also available in other electronic formats, and people with disabilities can now use a great deal of information that was formerly out of their reach.

Electronic catalogs have become standard features in most libraries, replacing card catalogs. This provides a great benefit for people with disabilities because an adapted computer terminal will allow a blind person or a person who can't manipulate file cards in a standard card catalog the ability to perform searches of a library's holdings from a computer terminal. The terminal may be publically accessible in the library, or it may be sitting on a student's desk in a dorm room.

ACCESS TO CAMPUSWIDE INFORMATION SYSTEMS

The campuswide information system is one of the latest developments in campus information automation. A college or university may provide their course catalog, schedule of classes, campus job bulletin, schedule of events, course requirements, required reading lists, and many other types of information through an online information system. The ability to access such a database is beneficial for all students and staff, but it offers particular benefits for blind and other print-handicapped individuals. Some students who have had to rely on others to read course schedules and class descriptions can now peruse college catalogs at their leisure through the online availability of such information.

ACCESS TO CD-ROMS

Many campus libraries offer database information via CD-ROMs. This is a great boon for students and staff with disabilities. The campus library must make available the necessary peripheral equipment and software so that individuals with disabilities can gain access to the CD-ROM collection. For example, the addition of a large-print software program can make CD-ROM dissertation abstract data accessible to students with low vision.

TECHNOLOGY THAT CREATES BARRIERS FOR PEOPLE WITH DISABILITIES

The same technology that frees people with disabilities can sometimes present them with new barriers to overcome. The increasing incorporation into software of graphic user interfaces (GUIs), in which information is accessed by using a mouse to click on graphic icons, has presented problems for some people with disabilities—especially blind people, who rely on screen readers to tell them what is displayed on a screen. A screen reader responds to text, not graphics. This has led to a call for all such icons to be clearly captioned with text and arranged in standard columns in order to be detectable by a screen reader and not confusing to the person using the screen reader. Not every software company has heeded that call, so libraries need to be aware of the concern when deciding between various products for their computer systems.

For people with learning disabilities, graphic user interfaces can be helpful or frustrating, according to the cognitive difficulties the person may have. Some people who have problems comprehending the printed word will benefit from the use of a GUI. Others who have problems processing visual or graphic information may be deterred by a system of icons. What should librarians do? If possible, they should offer access to the system through both a text and graphic interface. If a patron has difficulty with one, he or she can try the other. Since this may not always be possible, the staff should stand ready to explain how to gain access to the system in the simplest way possible.

Providing computer access to the library's catalog and various databases solves only part of the library's problem of how to provide access to all people. The vast majority of information in most libraries is still in the form of ink on paper, sitting in the stacks, out of reach for many people with disabilities. That does not seem likely to change soon. Although it is theoretically possible to scan the entire contents of the library and record them electronically, such a task—for the present at least—is not economically feasible or practical. And even when it becomes feasible, there may be copyright and other legal restrictions to providing such books in an easy-to-copy, easy-to-steal format. There are, however, a number of alternative formats for books.

BRAILLE

The most obvious alternative book format is Braille—a system of tactile printing developed by Louis Braille in the mid-nineteenth century as a way to educate blind children and provide them with a way to read the Bible. Braille, who lost his sight in a childhood accident, built his system around a six-dot cell, two dots across and three dots high. By raising various dots and leaving the others flat, the Braille system allows blind people to read by running their fingertips across the line, feeling each letter in succession.

The problem with Braille is that it is bulky and expensive to produce. Each letter must be large enough to distinguish by touch, and the paper has to be thick and stiff enough to retain the raised dots. That problem was lessened somewhat by the invention of Grade II Braille. In the original (Grade I) Braille, each letter is assigned a separate cell. Grade II Braille builds on that system by adding almost 200 additional dot symbols for frequently occurring words and word parts. For instance, instead of having three separate cells for the word *the*, there is only one. Instead of having five cells for the suffix *-ation*, there are only two. Grade II Braille somewhat reduces the bulk needed for Braille printing and also allows the reader to read more quickly.

The bulk problem is also mitigated by a process known as interpointing. Because Braille requires that paper be pressed into a format of raised dots, it is limited to one side of the page only. With interpointing, the paper is shifted so that the lines of raised dots on one side of the page are offset from the lines on the other side. That means the paper can be pressed from one side of the page, then from the other without interfering with the Braille type on the other side.

Despite such innovations, however, Braille is still a bulky method of printing, requiring several large, awkward volumes to hold the same information as one volume of an ink-on-paper text. Braille has other shortcomings as well. There is no way to use typography to help communicate information to the reader. Sighted readers take typography for granted—few even think about it. But boldfaced items, subheads, italics, different typefaces, and white space do not translate into a Braille document. There is one size, and in effect, one typeface all strung together. A sighted reader might skim through a selection, looking for typographical clues that will indicate an area of interest. Although there is a Braille code for such things as subheads, they are merely another set of dots, so they do not make that information stand out on the page the way bigger type or boldface print does for a sighted person.

In addition, Braille literacy may be on the decline, although this is an issue of some dispute within the blind community. Even at the height of its popularity, Braille was never used by all blind people. Now, according to some figures, less than 8 percent of the blind population is able to read it. Still, many blind people feel that Braille is the only format available that allows them to be truly literate. With recorded texts, blind people listen passively as books are read to them by third parties. With Braille, blind people interact with the words on a page, much as sighted readers do.

Recorded texts may have led to the current decline in Braille literacy. When Thomas Edison invented the phonograph, he saw it as a device for producing recorded books for blind people. But Edison's original idea would not be realized until more than 50 years later, in 1932, when the American Foundation for the Blind began recording books. The recorded books were immediately popular among blind people, many of whom had lost their sight later in life and therefore had not been schooled in Braille. The recorded texts have also become popular with sighted people who have problems holding books or turning pages.

Braille Transcription Center (BTC)

The Braille Transcription Center (BTC) is a center that produces instructional materials in Braille. It allows the California State University (CSU) system to provide blind students access to instructional materials in Braille at the same time as print-reading students.

The basic design of the BTC project is simple. Students, faculty, or staff located on a CSU campus send the instructional materials they want to have transcribed into Braille to the BTC. The information may be sent by conventional mail, overnight courier, fax, or electronically through the Internet. Once the instructional material has been received, the staff of the center converts the information into Braille. This task is accomplished by utilizing state-of-the-art, computer-based Braille production systems. All embossed documents are checked for formatting and transcription errors by a Braille transcriber certified by the Library of Congress. After the transcription process has been completed, the embossed documents are returned to the appropriate party by conventional mail or overnight courier.

Since the primary mission of the BTC is to provide Braille access in a timely manner, an outreach program is an important component of the project. The outreach program focuses on making students, faculty, and staff in the CSU system aware of the BTC and what their responsibilities are in making the program successful. Every effort is made to encourage and support the use of existing technologies such as fax machines and e-mail to expedite the transfer of information and materials. Emphasis is placed on the importance of submitting instructional materials to the BTC far enough in advance to allow for sufficient time to transcribe and return the instructional material by the desired date.

The final function of the BTC is as a resource. Technical support and training are provided to CSU campuses that already have on-site Braille production equipment. The BTC also conducts evaluations of computer-based technologies related to the Braille transcription process. All findings are documented and made available to other campuses in the CSU system.

This innovative project offers a solution to the problem of providing individualized instructional materials in Braille to students throughout the CSU system in a timely manner. The creation of the BTC not only provides an increased opportunity for students who use Braille to achieve, but it also has raised the CSU system's level of compliance with existing civil rights laws.

ENLARGED TEXT

Another book format for people who are vision impaired, as opposed to blind, is books with large-size print. Large print is also beneficial for many people with learning disabilities.

Type size is measured in units called points. The type in most books is 10 or 12 points. Type 14 point or larger is considered "large print." Most large-print books use 16- to 18-point type, however. The readability of large-print books depends on more than just the size of the type. The contrast between the ink and the paper, the amount of space between lines of type, and the simplicity of the typeface used also affect how accessible the book is for visually-impaired readers.

MICROFICHE, MICROFILM, AND CLOSED-CIRCUIT TELEVISIONS

Although large-print books have been available from commercial publishers since the 1960s, most books are not offered in that format. Two other technologies available for people with limited vision are books on microfilm or microfiche and closed-circuit television. In the first case, the book is recorded on microfilm or microfiche and the reader uses a microfilm or microfiche reading machine to enlarge it to the size desired. In the second, the actual book is spread out in front of a closed-circuit television camera, which displays it at the size desired on an adjacent screen (see Chapter 7).

One low-tech, inexpensive solution that can help low-vision patrons in a pinch is to have magnifying glasses available. For many patrons who are only trying to look up a brief item in a research book, a magnifying glass will provide all the help they need.

The library should also have a scanner with optical character recognition software in order to scan material and convert it into an electronic format. This can be connected to a Braille embosser so blind patrons can print copies of what they are working on, much as able-bodied library patrons can.

ALTERNATIVE FORMATS AND COPYRIGHT CONSIDERATIONS

One of the main issues determining the alternative formats that are available for people with disabilities is the economics of publishing. This was not a big issue when it came to reproducing books in Braille. The market for Braille books is not large enough to make it profitable to publish such books, so it is not a problem to allow a nonprofit organization to reproduce books in Braille, since it has little effect on the publisher's profit. Blind people are the only ones who read Braille, and they're not potential customers for regular ink-on-paper books.

Recorded books are a different story. Recorded books are of interest to both disabled and able-bodied people, and they are easily copied and "bootlegged." One of the ways such organizations as the National Library Service and Recording for the Blind and Dyslexic have been able to convince publishers to allow reproduction of their books on tape is to record the books on a nonstandard machine that requires a special machine for playback. Those special machines—which can only play tapes, not record them—are loaned out by the organizations to people certified as disabled. Although commercial publishers now also offer books on tape, for the most part these have been scaled-down versions of the original books, severely edited in order to fit on two or three cassettes.

The availability of books in an electronic, computer-accessible format faces copyright problems because the books can be easily copied with the push of a button. Still, more and more books are becoming available on audiotape and electronically on CD-ROMs and floppy disks. (In fact, the authors of this book insisted in their contract that it be made available in ASCII format on disk, for the same purchase price as the book.) How threatened are publishers? Maybe less than it appears at first glance. Most people, it seems, would still rather curl up with a book than read it on a screen.

AVAILABILITY OF LIBRARY INFORMATION

The in-house materials published by the library, such as guides to the library and brochures, should also be available in alternative formats. Audiotapes of these library publications can be made on a standard tape recorder. Large-print versions of computer-generated materials can be made by simply increasing the type size and printing out a few extra copies. They may also be included on a floppy disk for those patrons who prefer to have electronic versions.

The library also needs to have materials on how to use the library's adaptive technology available in alternative formats. These should include simple, step-by-step instructions on how to use the important features of that technology, similar to the operating instructions provided for all the library computers. This allows patrons with disabilities to be as independent as possible and lessens the need for direct staff involvement in explaining the system. In many cases, however, the library staff will have to retrieve materials from the stacks or other places that may be inaccessible to patrons with disabilities.

There are several sources of books and other materials available in formats accessible to disabled people. Two organizations that provide such material are the National Library Service (NLS) and Recording for the Blind and Dyslexic (RFB&D).

THE NATIONAL LIBRARY SERVICE

The NLS was established in 1931 as the result of the federal Pratt-Smoot Act, which guaranteed annual federal funding for the production and distribution of Braille books. Commercial publishers don't print books in Braille because the process is expensive and the demand is not sufficient to generate a profit. Such books would be so expensive that few libraries or blind people would be able to afford them. So the NLS—backed by a government subsidy—began printing and supplying Braille books to libraries and blind people. It also began exploring new ways to help deliver information to people with disabilities. The

NLS was the pioneer in developing audio recordings of books and in finding more efficient ways to produce Braille books and documents.

Through a network of regional libraries, the NLS collection is available for lending to qualified individuals and institutions, such as libraries, nursing homes, hospitals, and schools. It will also lend the equipment necessary to play book recordings that are not compatible with standard tape recorders. The titles in the NLS collection represent the popular literature of the day—books chosen for their appeal to a wide audience. The books available tend toward popular fiction, how-to books, biographies, and best-sellers. The NLS uses trained actors to read its books, and the quality is excellent. Although both Braille and recorded texts are available, recorded texts tend to outnumber those in the Braille format. *Braille Books* and *Talking Book Topics,* the two NLS catalog publications, are available free of charge from branch NLS libraries. A catalog of NLS publications is also available on CD-ROM.

To be eligible for NLS books, a person must have no better than 20/2000 vision in their better eye, even with correcting lenses, or have a visual field of less than a 20-degree angle. Even if a person does not meet that standard, they may still be eligible if a competent authority will certify

- Their vision disability prevents them from reading a standard printed page.
- They have a physical disability that prevents them from using standard printed materials.
- They have an organic dysfunction, which results in a reading disability that prevents them from reading printed materials in a usual manner.

A competent authority is defined to include doctors of medicine, doctors of osteopathy, ophthalmologists, optometrists, registered nurses, and therapists. In the absence of those authorities, certification may be made by a professional librarian or any person whose competence in a specific situation is acceptable to the Library of Congress. You can contact the NLS by telephone at 202-707-5100.

RECORDING FOR THE BLIND AND DYSLEXIC

If the National Library Service is the public library for people with disabilities, Recording for the Blind and Dyslexic is the research library. It is a nonprofit agency that specializes in audio recordings of educational material for students at all levels and of special texts for adult professionals. For students, RFB&D is often the only source for the books they need in their studies. RFB&D has an extensive library of recorded materials. It also has numerous volunteer readers and the ability to produce recordings of books "on demand." Students who want an audiotape of a book must submit two copies of the book to RFB&D. The books are then assigned to readers at one of the RFB&D studios.

There are a number of other differences between NLS and RFB&D. When RFB&D records a novel, it includes the page numbers. NLS does not. RFB&D also includes footnotes, descriptions of pictures and charts, and the bibliography. In other words, RFB&D attempts to include all the information included on the printed page.

In addition to audio recordings, RFB&D also offers for sale about 500 books in computer-readable form on IBM-, Macintosh- and Apple-formatted disks. Prices are in the $10 to $50 range.

With such an extensive service, RFB&D is strict about who qualifies for its help. Students wishing to use the RFB&D service must have their vision certified by a medical doctor. Printed catalogs of RFB&D recordings are available for purchase; inquiries may be made by a phone call to the RFB&D at 800-221-4792 to check on specific titles. In addition, a catalog of newly recorded material is issued quarterly on both audiotape and computer disk. The RFB&D catalog is also accessible by telenetting to r2d2.jvnc.net port 4445.

Both the NLS and RFB&D have regional recording studios around the country, and many of these have developed a specialty niche. The RFB&D studios in Boston and Philadelphia, for instance, are known for their science and technology transcriptions. The one in Washington, DC, has a reputation for foreign languages, and the one in New York for arts and science. The NLS studio in New York, on the other hand, is known for its recordings of history books and articles.

A directory of Braille and recorded texts is also available online through the Library of Congress Information System (LOCIS). In addition to the traditional online catalog of publications and other databases, LOCIS also has one for "Braille and Audio" publications, including those "In Process." You can find LOCIS on the World Wide Web at: http://lcweb.loc.gov/nls/nls.html.

BOOKS AVAILABLE ELECTRONICALLY

One of the earliest electronic publishing programs to make books available over the Internet (see Chapter 11) was the one instituted by a group called Project Gutenberg. Led by Michael Hart, Project Gutenberg has been a largely volunteer effort to take out-of-print books, put them into electronic format, and make them freely available on the Internet. Most of these are classics that are in the public domain. Available titles include the King James Version of the Bible and the works of William Shakespeare, John Milton, and Lewis Carroll. The collection can be found at several locations on the Internet, but the main repository is available by anonymous ftp from mrcnext.cso.uiuc.edu.

In an effort to be accessible to all, Project Gutenberg has chosen to store these books in plain document text (ASCII) and not to include any high-level formatting. While it does provide texts immediately accessible to anyone with a low-level text reader or word processor, many scholars complain that its usefulness is limited by not providing some of the format information so important and useful in printed materials.

Project Gutenberg is only one of several Internet-based providers of free texts. The Online Book Initiative, OBI, is another; it can be reached by anonymous ftp at world.std.com.

Most computers connected to the Internet will permit the use of ftp. From your system prompt, issue the command **ftp**, followed by the address of the computer to which you want to connect. For example, to reach Project Gutenberg, you would type: **ftp mrcnext.cso.uiuc.edu**, and when connected, you can log in as **anonymous** for your user name. The ftp will permit you to retrieve a document from a remote computer but will not support your reading of it until you have transferred it to your own machine.

Finding such collections of books and remembering how to access them is confusing for some people. Many gopher and Web sites have pointers to text resources, but these are so diverse and scattered that using them is discouraging. Several institutions and individuals attempt to maintain lists of this collection, and that is a help. Still there is no single catalog available. EASI maintains a Web page that provides users some idea of where to begin.

Commercial online services frequently have reference works available. As the customer is a paying user identifiable by a password, the providers have made license agreements with publishers of books, magazines, and newspapers to make these items available to their patrons. Similarly, many colleges have materials available, but they are limited by password to students and faculty.

Recording for the Blind and Dyslexic has recently begun providing electronic texts both in plain ASCII text and in formatted texts, including many computer manuals, computer programming books, and a number of reference works.

A WORD ABOUT LIBRARY STAFF

Training for the library staff will be similar to training for people in computer labs, as discussed in Chapter 3. Library patrons with disabilities need to feel that they are welcome in the library and that they are not a bother to the staff. Some individuals with disabilities, especially those making their first visit, may feel inhibited about using the library. Like all people, they need to be treated with respect.

Some staff people should be cross-trained in the adaptive computing technology, electronic information access, and library science in order to show patrons with disabilities how to use the technology and how to find what they want. In short, the staff has to be trained to be a partner in helping people with disabilities overcome whatever barriers they face in the libraries. The technology is the doorway for people who have been locked out too long. The library staff is there to help people with disabilities open that door.

CHAPTER 11

The Information Highway and the Information Hungry

T he Internet is a vast tangle of interconnected local and regional computer networks that connects millions of computers ranging from supercomputers to notebooks. It allows an almost instantaneous exchange of electronic data between computers. The Internet is growing rapidly in size—but even more rapidly in the number of users and in the quantity of information being transferred.

The Internet is the centerpiece of the Information Age. It carries up-to-the-second stock reports, and it exchanges data on local and international weather conditions. It connects the branches of a multinational corporation. It transmits the letter of a lonely freshman back home to Mother. Among its most eager and devoted users are people with disabilities.

Historically, people who have disabilities that make it difficult to use traditional texts have been starved for information. Some who are blind or vision impaired are not able to read print. Others with mobility impairments are unable to physically handle a book or piece of paper. Those with visual processing disorders can see the print, but have difficulty making sense of what seems to be a jumble.

While people with hearing impairments have no difficulty seeing print, they often experience a sense of isolation because they cannot share in general spoken conversation. The telephone does not help, unless there is a convenient relay system. The Internet can help overcome some of that isolation by providing deaf people the opportunity of sharing in casual contact with others.

The computer, with appropriate adaptations, provides a gateway to the Internet for many people with disabilities. It allows people with print impairments to use printed material stored in digital formats. For many people, this experience is both exciting and empowering. In the Information Age, power is no longer based on physical abilities, but rather on intellect.

How does the Internet help people with disabilities? First, it does for them what it does for others—it opens up a new world of information. But this time, people with disabilities are on equal footing with everyone else. A researcher who cannot hold a book to look up information can now use an adapted computer to access an electronic database and conduct research independently.

Second, it's a method of convenient and private conversation. A deaf man uses it to "chat" with a hearing friend, rather than using the phone and relay system. A mobility-impaired student accesses the library online catalog to check a book's availability before making a trip downtown to get it. A blind philosophy professor requires students to submit their papers by electronic mail rather than on paper, and his computer does the reading for him.

ELECTRONIC MAIL

Electronic mail greatly enhances both personal and professional communications. For those who are print impaired, it provides new freedom and privacy in sending and reading mail. One student said he wished he had e-mail available to him sooner, so he could have avoided the embarrassment of having a friend read him a "Dear John" letter from his girlfriend. People with hearing impairments now have a new communication channel between themselves and their hearing acquaintances that can bypass the relay networks and the need for an interpreter. Besides permitting a new level of privacy, e-mail is quick and convenient.

While e-mail is primarily a one-to-one communication medium, it can also facilitate interaction between groups of people. Internet discussion lists are essentially computerized mass-mailing systems. Each is operated from a specific computer somewhere on the Internet and uses a special mailing software called a list server.

With thousands of Internet discussion lists available, how do you find the ones that would most interest you? The easiest way may be through the recommendation of a friend. However, there are also sites on the Internet where lists of lists are kept and indexed. A comprehensive index is on the Web at http://www.lsoft.com/lists/listref.html. Discussion lists are far more significant than the casual reader will guess. They are powerful information tools. Discussion lists frequently carry questions about some problem, requests for information, or a plea for help in solving a technical difficulty. Usually, the list will provide several replies within a matter of hours from individuals with the identical need who have found a solution and are willing to share what they know. For people who cannot easily read manuals and special interest magazines, this becomes an invaluable resource.

EASI (Equal Access to Software and Information) sponsors several electronic discussion lists that focus on adaptive computing and information technology. The most general list, EASI, has several hundred subscribers, including both people with disabilities and others who are interested in facilitating access to information technology for people with disabilities. A second list, AXSLIB-L, is dedicated to helping libraries be more accessible to patrons with disabilities. These two discussion lists—and a number of other disability-related lists—are hosted on a computer at St. John's University. EASI also sponsors a special Internet discussion list on access in the fields of science, engineering, and math, EASI-SEM, which is hosted at the Rochester Institute of Technology. See Appendix B for information on how to subscribe to these discussion lists.

Some of the other topics of electronic mailing lists hosted at St. John's University include attention deficit disorder, chronic pain, amputees, families of people with disabilities, and mobility impairments, and there are many lists related to children with disabilities. DEAF-L is one of many deafness-related lists (it is hosted at listserv@siucvmb.bitnet). BLIND-L is a list on blindness (hosted at listserv@uafsysb.uark.edu). ADA-LAW is a discussion of the Americans with Disabilities Act (available through listserv@vm1.nodak.edu). The DO-IT Project at the University of Washington maintains a list of Internet disability resources including discussion lists, gophers, and World Wide Web sites. It is posted on the Web at http://weber.u.washington.edu/~doit/Brochures/internet_resources.html.

GOPHER AND THE WORLD WIDE WEB

Networked computers are both communication and storage devices. A computer can use the Internet to retrieve and utilize data stored at a remote computer. At one point, the networks were almost like a library full of books that were not catalogued or even organized. The need to impose some order on this body of information and simplify techniques for obtaining that information led to the creation of Internet navigation tools such as gopher and World Wide Web browsers. Gopher is primarily text-based and has been rapidly surpassed in popularity by the Web, which includes the ability to display graphics. (Graphics on the Web pose problems for some users with disabilities, however, and this problem, as well as how to design attractive and accessible Web pages, will be discussed later in this chapter.)

EASI is one of many organizations with a Web site devoted to disability issues. The EASI gopher is hosted at St. John's University and can be found at sjuvm.stjohns.edu. The EASI Web page at the Rochester Institute of Technology, http://www.rit.edu/~easi, has a focus on disabilities and information technology. Besides publications and resources related to adaptive computing, the EASI Web site focuses on education issues. Through the support of the National Science Foundation, EASI has provided many resources on access to science, engineering, and math at http://www.rit.edu/~easi/easisem.html.

As libraries are becoming more accessible to people with disabilities, EASI devotes increasing amounts of space to library access issues at http://www.rit.edu/~easi/lib.html. Information about distance learning workshops on adaptive computing that EASI conducts on the Internet is at http://www.rit.edu/~easi/workshops.html. Another page provides information about the ADA and information technology. All pages, of course, have links to other relevant Web resources around the world.

The University of Washington DO-IT project, which prepares disabled high school students for studying science in college, maintains an extensive Web presence at http://weber.u.washington.edu/~doit.

The Trace Research and Development Center located at the University of Wisconsin has another important Web site at http://www.trace.wisc.edu. Trace is a leader in research and development of various computer and information technology systems for people with disabilities. Dr. Gregg Vanderheiden is a recognized leader in both research and in influencing industry to become more aware of disability issues when they design new systems and technology.

The Boston public television station, WGBH (http://www.wgbh.org), is widely recognized for its leadership in providing access to television. It is a leader in both captioning for the deaf and in providing video description services for the blind. It is also trying to lead in the area of access to multimedia and has sponsored the National Center for Accessible Media with its Web page at http://www.boston.com/wgbh/pages/ncam/ncamhome.html.

The Library of Congress National Library Service for the Blind and Physically Handicapped is another important Internet resource. Its Web page at http://lcweb.loc.gov/nls/nls.html has its entire catalog online. For the first time, blind library patrons can use the catalog without assistance. The NLS Web page also maintains a large list of Internet resources that provide electronic texts. Using this page, an individual can locate thousands of texts and either read them online or download for later enjoyment.

Recording for the Blind and Dyslexic (RFG&D) provides an online catalog at http://www.rfbd.org. RFB&D is the world's largest repository and provider of books for vision-impaired college students and professionals. These books have traditionally been audio recordings, but many of them are now in electronic format. At this point, neither RFB&D nor NLS delivers books over the Internet. The need to protect copyrighted materials from being accessed illegally is one of the barriers. Book availability will be hastened by the recent legislation enabling any nonprofit organization to produce textbooks in alternative formats for people with disabilities. However, the need to protect those books from unauthorized use will continue.

Yahoo is one of the Web's most popular features for helping users locate information on any topic anywhere in the world. It has a page on disability resources at http://www.yahoo.com/text/Society_and_Culture/Disabilities. Webable is a Web site at http://www.yuri.org/webable/. It maintains a detailed online and searchable database of Internet resources and those that can be searched by topic or by geographical location. It provides links to Web sites on blindness, vision impairments, cognitive impairments, deafness, hearing impairments, and others. Webable provides pointers to manufacturers of adaptive software and hardware, including both the small adaptive technology companies and larger corporations such as Apple, Digital Equipment Corporation, and IBM.

The National Rehabilitation Information Center (NARIC) at http://www.naric.com/naric provides useful information concerning particular disabilities. The project is funded by the National Institute on Disability and Rehabilitation Research. The U.S. Department of Health and Human Services page is at http://www.os.dhhs.gov/, and information from the Social Security Administration is available at http://www.ssa.gov. The National Science Foundation funds several projects to increase the representation of disabled people in science education and technical professions. Many of these projects are linked at http://www.rit.edu/~easi/easisem.html.

WEB ACCESS PROBLEMS FOR PEOPLE WITH DISABILITIES

The special power of the Web is its ability to transmit pictures and sounds and to display text with specialized formatting instructions. Computers have been able to handle sounds and pictures for a long time. But sounds and pictures both take enormous amounts of disk space to store, and equally large amounts of network bandwidth to transmit. For that reason, the Internet was seldom used for transmitting either pictures or sound. In recent years, however, disk memory, computer speed, and network bandwidth have all increased rapidly. This makes it more feasible to transmit pictures and sounds over computer networks. Many of the advantages of this technology are obvious, but there are some disadvantages as well. There are at least four specific problem areas for individuals with disabilities:

- Because the computer display is often richer and more complicated, it can be disturbing for persons with visual processing disorders.

- More graphically oriented Web browsers, like many other graphics-based software, may require the use of the mouse to navigate the Web. Some people with motor impairments may find this impossible.
- The use of sound to convey content may leave hard-of-hearing and deaf people with no way to access information.
- The use of pictures to convey information may create a barrier for vision-impaired individuals.

The technology to solve these problems is available. What it requires is careful and thoughtful design. Instead of creating a system that requires the end user to conform to the format ideas of the system creator, systems should be built to permit as many user-definable features as possible.

Often, many of the graphic elements in a display are decorative. For individuals who learn better from a cleaner, less complex presentation, the ability to "turn off" such enhancements would facilitate their use of the Web while not requiring others to forego the pleasure of the graphics. Even at today's transmission speeds, the use of extensive graphics may slow down the retrieval of information. Many able-bodied users may also prefer to turn off decorative graphics in order hurry things along.

For people who have trouble manipulating a mouse, or who find the mouse inconvenient, there is a type of software called mouse keys that permits the use of the arrows to simulate mouse movements. The Web browser that permits alternative ways of navigating the links on the Web will be useful to the broadest spectrum of users.

When the Web transmits sounds, the function of the sound will determine how it is adapted for the deaf user. If the sound is sound effects or sound enhancement, a tag saying what it is will fill the needs of both deaf people and people whose computers lack audio capability. If the sound is carrying the content of the information, there should be the possibility of supplying captions. Even if the information provider does not include the captions, the Web system and browser should have the capability of its being added at a later time.

Similarly, the adaptation of pictures and graphics for vision-impaired users will be influenced by the function of those non-text items. Text browsers normally insert the word "image" where there is a picture. The *alt-text* feature in HTML (Hypertext Markup Language) will let the producer insert a brief tag such as "logo" or some other description. This is helpful for blind Web users as well as for others using text browsers or who have the graphics mode turned off on their browser in order to speed up transmission. However, if the graphics element is an important part of the content, there should be at least the possibility of adding a text description.

An example of this is the White House Web page. In its early version, it displayed a picture of the White House that served both as a picture and as a directory. The user could point to the part of the building he or she wanted to know more about, and this brought up textual information about the uses of that area. However, blind users were not able to make sense out of this, and eventually, the graphics-based directory was changed. The page now provides two systems to access the directory, a clickable map and a text listing of the rooms in the building.

One major problem people with vision impairments encounter with graphics is when visual information is presented using a picture of the text rather than the electronic equivalent of the letters and words. A word processor or screen reader can recognize letters and words in the standard digital form. But if the information provider puts a picture of those same letters and words on the page, the computer only sees it as colors and shapes. The software that turns the writing on a computer screen into synthetic speech for a screen reader needs to know that it is dealing with letters and words in order for it to make the screen reader "talk." For the blind user, textual content that is transmitted as graphics is useless.

In 1996, the Department of Justice's Office of Civil Rights in San Francisco issued a letter of finding, Docket Number 09-95-2206. A student had complained about not being provided adequate access to the World Wide Web. The resolution stated that the student should be provided with the best Web access tools for blind users. While the decision focused on providing client browsers for the student, there would also appear to be a requirement for creating Web pages that are reasonably accessible at the server end as well. The decision was based on Section 504 of the 1973 Rehabilitation Act and on Title II of the Americans with Disabilities Act (see Chapter 2). Certainly, the decision insisted that printed college course materials must be rendered in alternate format, and this must extend to accessible electronic resources. Using design principles that enhance universal access is important if schools, colleges, libraries, and other public facilities are to avoid legal confrontations.

HTML: HYPERTEXT MARKUP LANGUAGE

The International Standards Organization (ISO) is trying to reach an agreement on format codes for electronic texts. SGML (Standard Generalized Markup Language) is its set of tags for standard formatting, and it is receiving increasing acceptance. HTML (Hypertext Markup Language) is a variant of SGML. HTML is aimed at the transmission and display of electronic materials over computer networks, and it is also receiving increasing acceptance. Much of the material on the Web is in HTML format. ICADD, the International

Committee on Accessible Document Design, is working with ISO to ensure that the HTML standards include tags that will enable computer systems to extract information from stored electronic texts.

The advantage of HTML over the use of plain text is that Web browsers can use a large number of formatting features. Headers can appear in larger type. Words can be displayed in bold format. Graphics and other non-text information can be combined with the text material. It also allows the information provider to include pointers or links to other pages of text. This feature results in a complex World Wide Web of information. Careful use of HTML permits the provider to create an attractive display, mixing text, pictures, and decorative graphics. It also provides a standard that will permit a blind user to get the maximum benefit from the content.

Gregg Vanderheiden of the Trace Research and Development Center says a truly accessible network display system must have three components to be accessible to users with disabilities:

- The content must be stored in an accessible format (HTML meets this need).
- The transmission system must carry all the information possible and not alter or strip out important data.
- The equipment used to view the information must be "user friendly" for individuals with disabilities.

Designing an accessible Web page means increasing its availability for everyone—not only for people with disabilities. Some Web sites are designed for only one version of a particular browser. This may enable maximizing its features, but it limits the number of visitors to the site. Some Web users have low-speed connections, and heavy graphics are annoyingly slow. Others, even with good connectivity, turn off graphics to further speed up their Web access. Some visitors may be blind and not benefit from heavy graphics. Learning-disabled individuals may find complex graphics confusing and disorienting. Deaf users will not be able to benefit from audio presentations. Good design will be a compromise between maximizing available Web features and rapid, clear conveyance of information. The purpose of most Web pages should be to communicate and not merely to impress the visitor.

Web browsers and HTML are both evolving so rapidly that it is useless to present detailed instructions on writing accessible HTML code. However, there are five Web sites that regularly update their guidelines for creating HTML for the needs of disabled users.

- The Trace Research and Development Center: http:/www. trace.wisc.edu
- DO-IT Project: http://weber.u.washington.edu

- Webable: http://www.yuri.org/webable/
- WGBH: http://www.wgbh.orga
- The World Wide Web Consortium disability page: http://www.w3.org/pub/WWW/Disabilities/

A basic list of guidelines:

- Avoid image maps or provide an alternate text list.
- Use *alt-text* tags for images.
- Provide description for significant graphics.
- Avoid tables or provide alternatives.
- Provide text for audio clips.
- Provide description for video clips.
- Test the page on your browser with graphics turned off.

Keep your Web page design simple, and focus on communicating to the largest audience possible. Remember, Internet users are often impatient and may quickly go elsewhere to find what they want. Making the design readily accessible to persons with disabilities will ensure that they will be quickly and readily accessible to all users.

ELECTRONIC PUBLISHING AND ACCESS TO ELECTRONIC TEXTS

As electronic mail discussion groups became more popular, people began to write electronic newsletters on a variety of topics. Before long, this evolved into electronic publishing, which made books, magazines, and newspapers available online.

Scholars and researchers have long sought faster ways to get the results of their work published and into the hands of their readers. While electronic journals and electronic mail make rapid publication possible as never before, many of these publications have had difficulty in achieving academic recognition and acceptance. Those that combine the speed of the Internet with traditional care and accuracy in publication, and which also include the use of e-mail for peer review, are gradually gaining ground.

Information Technology and Disabilities is a quarterly, peer-reviewed electronic journal focused on adaptive computing and access to information technology for individuals with disabilities. Tom McNulty, a librarian at New York University, developed the concept for it in the summer of 1993. By the fall, an international board of editors—all friends and supporters of EASI—was in place, and a call for articles was distributed on the Internet. By January 1994, articles had been received and reviewed by professionals in relevant fields. Several hundred individuals had subscribed electronically, and at the end of the month, the first issue was sent on the Internet to readers in several countries. The fall issue of 1994 was a special volume related to access issues in the fields of science, engineering, and mathematics. The fall issue in 1995 was devoted to making libraries and electronic information in libraries more accessible to patrons with disabilities. Back issues of this journal can be found on EASI's Web page at http://www.rit.edu/~easi/itd.html.

A few organizations that produce print journals also make them available freely on the Internet. EDUCOM posts the *EDUCOM REVIEW* on its Web page at http://www.educom.edu. It also sends out an e-mail publication, *Edupage*, three times each week, summarizing news about computing.

AAAS, the American Association for the Advancement of Science, regularly posts its publication, *Science*, at gopher.aaas.org.

Although the line between a journal and magazine may not always be clear, there is a long list of magazines on the Internet too. Many have been created for electronic dissemination, but there are others that appear both in print and electronically. Many commercial magazines are accessible through paid commercial online services or over the Internet by subscription. A good source for magazines available on the Internet is the Electronic Newsstand at http://www.enews.com.

Although electronic publishing represents a significant change in publication and distribution, for print-impaired people it is an amazing revolution.

DISTANCE LEARNING

Recent advances in computers and in telecommunications have created revolutions in the fields of educational technology and distance learning. The name change from "distance education" to the more current "distance learning" is more than mere educational correctness. Distance learning encompasses a wide range of technologies and different educational systems. The traditional correspondence course still exists, as does the one-way radio or television class, but both force the student into a fairly isolated and passive mode. Modern technologies make it possible for much more interaction between teacher and students and between students. It is this movement of the learner into the active center of the process that led to the change in terminology.

Many colleges and universities are integrating electronic mail into education both for distance learning and to enhance the accessibility of classroom teachers. While Internet discussion lists permit mail to be part of a group activity, the computer conference system provides a better group setting. The potential for mainstreaming people with disabilities in distance learning settings is great.

Using computer-mediated education, the Rochester Institute of Technology (RIT) in Rochester, New York, and Gallaudet University in Washington, DC, ran a pilot project to demonstrate that this teaching method would work over the Internet. Several hundred miles separate the two schools. Almost all of the participating students from Gallaudet, a liberal arts school for the deaf, were deaf. Several of the RIT students were hearing impaired, the teacher was blind, and the remaining students had no known physical disability. The system worked as well as it had for students living in the same geographic community.

The computer conferencing system used in that particular model was VAX Notes by the Digital Equipment Corporation. It is an asynchronous system, but in spite of that, participants still had a sense of interacting with one another. The fact that it is asynchronous meant that students had an opportunity to think and reflect before they wrote. One student remarked that in class she got tongue-tied, but in the computerized conference she lost much of her shyness. The teacher and many of the students found they had more interaction than in many college classes with 40 or more students. Another class member said that he liked the conference because he felt he was judged by the content of his remarks and not by appearances.

Many colleges are providing courses through the Internet. Several of these have noted the potential to serve the needs of students with disabilities. Individual students with disabilities have taken classes at a number of schools, but no concerted program or research project has yet been established in this area. Considering the widespread interest and the escalation of distance-delivered courses, such a program is sure to emerge.

Besides regular college classes, the Internet is home to other kinds of distance learning experiences. EASI has been offering a workshop on adaptive computing using e-mail as the delivery mechanism. Adapt-It is a three-week course aimed at institutions and information providers that introduces the topics of adaptive computing and access to information technology. The purpose is to help organizations provide a systematic approach to making their computer and information systems accessible to students and professionals with disabilities. Between January 1994 and July 1995, more than 500 participants from 21 countries spread over 6 continents participated in the workshop. These have included students, government officials, professors, adaptive computing researchers, librarians, and people from private business. The diversity of participants has made this an interesting example of what distance learning can be.

DISTANCE LEARNING AND STUDENTS WITH DISABILITIES

If a school is using distance learning technology to deliver a course to a classroom at a remote location, the school providing the instruction is responsible to see that the remote site meets accessibility requirements, even if that site is not owned by the school. If the distance-delivery technology itself prohibits a student with a disability from participating in a class, the school may have to alter its program to remove that barrier. Schools are only required to make "reasonable accommodations," and the law leaves the school a great deal of latitude in how that is accomplished.

Television and videos frequently create barriers for both hearing-impaired and vision-impaired individuals. Captioning for people with hearing impairments is one obvious—but rather expensive—solution. If a video is being shown at a school location rather than being watched at home, using an interpreter may be an acceptable—but less adequate—alternative. Descriptive audio for blind people is an equivalent solution for vision-impaired students. Some videos and some television programs—especially those on the Public Broadcasting System—have descriptive audio.

If program presenters are trained and thoughtful, they can often discuss visual material in such detail that special adaptations become redundant. For example, a teacher may repeat what is being written on the board. In situations where teachers use captioning or repetition of what they are writing, all students learn better. Complex graphics and diagrams may not lend themselves to verbal descriptions. In such cases, the materials should be put in Braille or raised graphics for vision-impaired students. This requires planning and forethought on the part of both the teacher and the distance learning staff.

Audio materials, tapes, and phone conferences pose a barrier for deaf students. Possible solutions could include an interpreter taking detailed or verbatim notes on the audio material and making the notes available in print along with any other convenient method that allows deaf students to interact with the teacher on this material. This might be through the use of a phone and TDD or through electronic mail.

The software required by the course should be compatible with adaptive technology. The content should not rely on graphics as the method of conveying information. Where graphics are central to the content, as is the case in some scientific and technical fields, that material should be provided in an alternate format, such as Braille, descriptive audio, or captioning of computer audio.

The Information Age is rapidly changing the world. It promises to be as significant in its impact as was the printing press. While that invention increased the gulf between the print disabled and the rest of society, the digitizing of information is building a bridge across the gulf. It is important that the advent of new technologies be guided with a social concern. Many fear that this revolution will widen the gap between those with more education and those with less. However, networked computers are having the effect of decentralizing power. If we continue to pay attention to the potential and development of electronic information, the Information Age can be one of inclusion rather than of exclusion.

CHAPTER 12

Sensitivity and So Much More

Sometimes, attitude is everything. Remember when you were a child, and you'd say something to your mother, and you'd get in trouble "not for what you said, but for how you said it"? She wasn't criticizing the words you were saying, she was getting after you for your smart-alecky attitude. More than the words we say or the actions we take, the way in which we speak and act is important. The tone of our voices, the expressions on our faces, and the gestures we make all combine to reflect our attitudes about the people around us.

One of the most difficult barriers people with disabilities face is the negative attitudes and perceptions of others. Sometimes those attitudes are deep-rooted prejudices, based in ignorance and fear. Sometimes they are just unconscious misconceptions that result in impolite or thoughtless acts by otherwise well-meaning people. In either case, they form an obstacle to acceptance and full participation in society for a person with a disability.

Disability is often perceived as a yes-or-no proposition. You're either disabled or you're not. The truth is, disability is a continuum. At one end are perfect people (there aren't many of those around), and at the other end are people with severe impairments. Most of us fall somewhere in the middle. But we're all people, and we all want and deserve to be treated with respect and dignity. The basic rule—if there must be one—is to treat a person who happens to have a disability the very same way that you would treat anyone else. Be polite. Be friendly. Act *normal.*

My very best friend just happens to be in a wheelchair. Now, this friend of mine is very bright, very decent, very funny, very loyal—and a basic curmudgeon. He's got his good qualities, and he's got his bad qualities. Just like you and me. He's not wonderful because he's disabled and he's "managed to overcome so much." He's wonderful because he's my friend. So, how do I act around him? I act normal. Sometimes I say, "Let's go for a walk." I know perfectly well that the last time he went for a walk was about 10 years ago, but it's not bad to use such an expression when talking to people in wheelchairs. They know what you mean, and you're not being insensitive. You're just asking to share their company. You also shouldn't have any problem saying, "Do you see what I mean?" to a blind person. They understand what you're talking about, and if there's any uncomfortable feeling on your part, that comes from you being uncomfortable with the person's disability—not the person being uncomfortable with your language.

When my friend and I go for a walk, sometimes we come to a hill. When that happens, sometimes I ask if he wants a push. Sometimes he asks for a push. In either case, he tells me what he wants, and I act accordingly. For all the time we've spent together during the last eight years, and as comfortable as we've become with one another, I still respect his right to control his own body and movements. I know that he'll tell me if he wants assistance, and I never grab his chair and start moving it without his consent.

The main point is that there is no unusual etiquette about holding open a door, carrying a package, or even giving a push. The etiquette is exactly the same as it is with everyone we come in contact with. In the course of our daily lives, we all give and take a little help from our friends. That's all you need to do around disabled people. Offer, give, and take the very same things that you would in any other situation.

SOME SPECIAL CONSIDERATIONS

If you're not used to being around people with disabilities, there are a few things that you can offer and do to make things a little easier for them.

- Don't ever assume that a person with a disability needs your help. Always offer—and get an affirmative response—before acting.
- Make eye contact and talk directly to the person, not to the person's companion.
- Avoid actions and words that suggest that the person should be treated differently.
- Treat people with disabilities with the same respect and consideration that you have for everyone else—they *are* just like everyone else.

Vision Impairments

When you talk with a blind person, you might want to be more descriptive than you usually are. Point out odd room configurations, tell the person where an empty chair is, mention any clutter in the area. Try to help orient people, and definitely let them know of any hazards. You should mention it when you're heading toward a step, stairway, or escalator, and tell them the position of equipment and other objects on a desk or in a room.

Unless you know otherwise, assume that the person's hearing is just fine, and speak in a normal voice. Offer to read written information, and feel free to paraphrase when it's appropriate.

If you are asked to guide a person with a vision impairment, offer your arm. Never grab a person's arm or attempt to physically direct a person without express permission. The exception to that rule is if the person is walking into an immediate danger.

Learning Disabilities

Most people who have learning disabilities never let the people around them know it. As our society has become more aware of people with disabilities of all kinds, there is less embarrassment and stigma attached to learning disabilities. But, there are still people who never feel the need to mention their disability.

The greatest percentage of learning disabilities are due to visual or aural processing disorders. Many learning disabilities affect attention span and a person's ability to concentrate. When you talk with a person with a learning disability, the most important thing is not to make assumptions. Don't assume that the person is not listening just because you get no oral or visual feedback. If you are not sure that the person is listening, ask if he or she understands or agrees with what you're saying. Facial expressions that lead you to think the person is not listening may just mean that the person is concentrating or evaluating what you are saying.

Don't assume that you have to explain everything to people with learning disabilities. They do not necessarily have a problem with general comprehension. Do be willing to re-explain the information that you're presenting. Do offer to read or paraphrase written material for a person who seems to be having trouble understanding it.

Mobility Impairments

People with mobility impairments generally fall into four different groups. Some use wheelchairs. Some use motorized scooters. Some use crutches or walking canes. And some have impaired hand or arm movement, due either to missing fingers, hands, or arms, or due to diseases such as arthritis or cerebral palsy.

When you're working or talking with people in wheelchairs or people who use motorized scooters, try sitting down or crouching next to the person, to put yourself at their approximate height. Many people in wheelchairs end up with stiff necks at the end of the day because they've spent so many hours looking up to talk to people. It is also friendlier and has an equalizing effect to be at eye level with the person you are speaking with, rather than to be looking down at that person. Be sure that in your attempt to get at eye level with a person in a wheelchair or scooter, you're not bending over the person or are crouched so low that the person has to look down on you.

Never lean on a person's wheelchair or scooter. A wheelchair is personal space, and just as you would not be comfortable with a stranger or coworker touching your clothes or face, a person who uses a wheelchair will probably be uncomfortable with others leaning on the wheelchair.

For people with limited or no use of their hands and arms, offer to carry items and open doors.

Be aware of what is accessible and what is not accessible to people in wheelchairs, on scooters, and those who use crutches. Since the Architectural Barriers Act was put in place, society as a whole has become aware that we must have ramps available anytime there are stairs in a building. But accessibility goes deeper than that.

One college in California has what is meant to be an accessible women's restroom. The stalls have been widened, there is a wash basin at chair height, and there is even a mirror at chair height. But only women who have arms at least four feet long can get out of the restroom without the help of another person. If a person pulls her chair up close enough to reach the door handle, she is blocking the door with her own chair, making it impossible to proceed.

If you know of "accessible" places that really aren't, notify your school administration and individuals who might need the information. Be alert to ramps that are so steep that they're too hard for many people to use without assistance and rooms that meet legal requirements of accessibility but are hard to navigate, and note any types of danger that exist.

Speech Impairments

Learn to be a listener, and learn to be patient. These are both good qualities when you talk to anyone, but they are especially important when you're talking or working with a person with a speech impairment.

Don't complete sentences for a person, unless he or she looks to you for help. Let a person who stutters take the time to say what he or she wants to say. Be patient and listen carefully to a person who has slow or garbled speech. Don't pretend that you understand what a person is saying if you don't understand, just to be polite. Ask the person to repeat what he or she said. It is insulting to nod in agreement and pretend that you understand a person if you don't. That sends the message that you really don't believe the person has anything of value to say. People with speech impairments know that other people may have difficulty understanding what they are saying, and they are willing to repeat their comments.

Ask the person to spell or write down a word if you're not sure what is being said—but do this sparingly. Do not limit your conversation with a person who has a speech impairment to note writing. Accord people with speech impairments the respect that you give to everyone else. Give them the respect of really listening to what they have to say.

Hearing Impairments

Some deaf people can read lips. Some people have limited hearing. When you're communicating with a person with a hearing impairment, be sure to face that person so that he or she can see your lips and your facial expressions. This helps people who are reading lips, and also gives clues as to what you are communicating. Slow the rate at which you talk when speaking to a person with a hearing impairment, and increase the level of your voice, if that is appropriate. Communicate by writing notes, if that is necessary.

When you're with people with any type of disability, take their cues on how they do things, and react accordingly. In general, people will ask for your help if they want it. They'll repeat their ideas if necessary and will ask you to repeat yours if they need to hear your comments more than once.

A Note about Service Dogs

Universe is a beautiful and lovable pure-bred golden retriever. People just can't keep their hands off him. Because Universe is a service dog, he's allowed in all kinds of places that most dogs aren't. But Universe's lovability can be a problem. He works for a living, and distractions not only keep him from his immediate job, they also spoil his training and make it a liability to take him into restaurants, department stores, the classroom, and other public places.

It took two years and $7,000 to train Universe to follow 86 different commands. Universe can get his owner's shoes, pick up things that have been dropped on the floor, pull a wheelchair, and turn lights on and off. But, for all his training, and even though he seems almost human in the way he understands those 86 commands, Universe is still a dog. And a few unintended breaches in Universe's routine and training can have a devastating impact on Universe and his owner.

There are far too many stories of sad owners who have had to give up their dogs because friends, coworkers, and even complete strangers have interfered so much in the dog's routine that it no longer followed its training.

A social, service, or signal dog that does not obey commands cannot do what it was trained to do. That often means that the dog must be given up in favor of another dog that can do the job of helping his owner. This is a tragedy for the person losing a loving companion, and a hardship because the person's independence is often tied to the jobs that the dog can perform. It is also a terrible waste of training and resources.

There are four kinds of specialty training that working dogs can receive. Dogs can be trained as guide dogs, social dogs, signal dogs, or service dogs. The law allows guide, signal, and service dogs to enter all places that accept the general public. For years, the most commonly seen service dog has been a guide dog, used by a person who is blind. The dog will help its owner cross streets and navigate both indoors and outdoors.

Social dogs are trained to provide unconditional love to their owners. Social dogs are usually placed with autistic or retarded children and adults. Social dogs do not have the same legal rights as guide, service, and signal dogs, and they are generally not allowed into all public places.

Signal dogs are trained for people with hearing impairments. They perform tasks such as signaling that there is knocking at the door and warning of dangers such as fire.

Service dogs are trained to provide a variety of tasks for people with physical disabilities. They retrieve objects, press elevator buttons, and carry things.

There are a few things to keep in mind when you come in contact with a working dog.

- Never pet the dog without first asking the owner's permission—and then don't be surprised if the owner refuses. The dog has been trained to go to one owner for attention, and the bond between the owner and dog must not be compromised. The dog is praised for tasks he performs, and he is generally not coddled or played with at work—affection and play are usually reserved for off-hours at home. In any case, it must come from the owner. A dog that refuses to follow his owner's commands becomes a liability rather than an asset.
- Never feed the dog. This is probably the single most disruptive thing that an outsider can do with a working dog. The dog must associate food with his owner. If the dog is fed by other people, he will eventually stop following his owner's instructions. Also, most working dogs are on a planned and nutritionally sound diet, including dog treats that are given throughout the day. It's important that working dogs stay healthy and fit, and a little leftover pizza from your lunch does not help the working dog in any way.
- Do not talk to a working dog, and try to avoid eye contact. Working dogs are generally very intelligent, and they seem to know when you're talking about them. They also seem to know that talking will lead to a pat on the head, a scratch behind the ear, and maybe even a full belly rub—all nice contact between a dog and a human, but none of which helps the working dog and his owner maintain their relationship.

APPENDIX A

Model Campuses and Libraries

MODEL UNIVERSITY CAMPUSES

Successful adaptive computing programs for students and staff who are disabled have been established at the University of California, Los Angeles; the University of Missouri–Columbia; the University of New Orleans; Southern Connecticut State University; and the University of Washington. Their programs are described in the following sections.

University of California, Los Angeles (UCLA)

At UCLA, the responsibility for computer and information accessibility is shared by campus computing facilities, information providers (including the library), and departments. Recognizing the need for a central coordinating unit for these access concerns, the university's chancellor established the Disabilities and Computing Program (DCP) in 1987 as a permanent campuswide program, with an organizational base in the Office of Academic Computing's Microcomputer Support Office (the DCP began in 1984 under the auspices of Social Sciences Computing). The mission of the DCP reflects this campuswide focus of information technology accessibility:

> The Mission of the UCLA Disabilities and Computing Program (DCP) is to facilitate the integration of adaptive computing technology into the areas of instruction, research, and employment at UCLA, to benefit students, faculty, and staff with disabilities, and to provide campus-wide coordination and support for access to computers, local area networks, and on-line information resources by people with disabilities.

Computer and information accessibility requires ongoing coordination with a number of service providers on campus. The DCP works closely with its key partners, including the Chancellor's Advisory Committee on Disability, the ADA and 504 Office, the Office for Students with Disabilities, the Medical Center's Rehabilitation Center, Campus and Medical Center Human Resources, the UCLA Library, and the DCP's parent organization, the Office of Academic Computing and Microcomputer Support Office.

The DCP is staffed by a program coordinator, an assistant coordinator, and a usability analyst. The DCP budget includes annual funding for computer hardware and software to keep current with the state-of-the-art developments in adaptive computer technology.

Services for Students

The DCP provides the following services to UCLA students with disabilities (both permanent and temporary disabilities).

- Students are trained in the use of adaptive computer technologies as compensatory tools to enhance academic independence and productivity, including: reading machines, voice recognition, large-screen software and displays, voice synthesis, and Braille screen displays and printers.
- The DCP collaborates with the Office for Students with Disabilities (OSD), teaching assistants, and faculty on computer-based exam taking and note taking.
- The DCP collaborates with OSD on the production of instructional print materials in accessible formats for students with print impairments. Textbooks and related course information (including those in foreign languages) are optically scanned and converted into Braille print or computer files for voice output for students who are blind. A joint project with OSD's Learning Disabilities Program provides students with learning disabilities access to course materials on computer files that can be read with both voice synthesis and word highlighting for improved reading comprehension.
- The program has an equipment loaner pool, including laptop computers, for students to learn and evaluate adapted computer equipment prior to purchasing their own. Loaner laptop computers are also used for exams and in-class note taking.
- The DCP supports students' funding applications to the state Department of Rehabilitation for student-owned computer systems by writing letters of technology needs assessment.
- The DCP works with departmental computing support coordinators to ensure that students with disabilities have equal access to campus instructional computer labs.

Services for Staff and Faculty with Disabilities

The DCP provides the following services to UCLA staff and faculty with disabilities (both permanent and temporary disabilities), including teaching and research assistants:

- Staff and faculty can be trained in the use of adaptive computer technologies as compensatory tools to enhance independence and productivity in the workplace, including: reading machines, voice recognition, large-screen software and displays, voice synthesis, and Braille screen displays and printers.
- Ergonomic support is provided for employees with keyboard- or mouse-related repetitive strain injuries, including carpal tunnel syndrome. The DCP works closely with its partner, the Occupational Therapy department of the UCLA Medical Center's Rehabilitation Center. The DCP provides technical consulting to the occupational therapists who provide employees with ergonomic worksite evaluations.
- An equipment and software loaner pool, including laptop computers, is maintained for employees to learn and evaluate adapted computer equipment prior to a departmental purchase.
- The DCP coordinates with UCLA's ADA and 504 Office and the university's Reasonable Accommodation Fund to assist departments in the purchase of adaptive computer equipment for employees.
- The DCP works closely with the employee's departmental computing support coordinator in support of all the adaptive computer services.

Services to the Community

The DCP provides one-time consultations to people with disabilities and to other interested parties in the community. This includes equipment demonstrations and general consultation on potential adaptive computing technology strategies. The DCP does not provide ongoing support to community members who are not part of UCLA, but they do provide referrals to organizations that can offer ongoing services. For people outside of the Los Angeles area, the DCP refers them to local community organizations.

Access to Campuswide Information Resources

Public print information resources at UCLA, as at all universities, are increasingly available in electronic form. When online information resources are designed to a universal standard, new educational and employment opportunities become available to people with print disabilities. At UCLA, the DCP participates in work groups that design centralized online information resources to help insure that they are accessible and usable for all users:

- UCLA's campuswide information system, InfoUCLA. A partnership between Library Information Services, the Office of Academic Computing's Microcomputer Support Office, and the DCP works to ensure that InfoUCLA is fully usable by people with print impairments. An emphasis on preserving document structure through the use of SGML (Standard Generalized Markup Language) supports the conversion of key campus data, including the catalog and schedule of classes, into accessible document standards, including those based on the ICADD (International Committee on Accessible Document Design) SGML DTD (document type definition).
- The next generation of the UCLA Library online system, Orion2. The new system will move from a character-based to a graphical environment, presenting new challenges for print-impaired users. The DCP collaborated with the library in the development of a disability access specification for the design of the new system.
- Bruin Online, the campus e-mail and Internet access package. Bruin On-line, a project of the Office of Academic Computing, offers the UCLA community unprecedented access to information resources from home, school, or work. As a set of graphical Internet client software, the new package poses new challenges to the print impaired, unlike the previous character-based e-mail and Internet services. The DCP researches and supports character-based client software that offers the same functionality as Bruin On-line. At the same time, the DCP evaluates graphical screen access programs (screen readers) that can provide access to the graphical Bruin On-line clients.

Usability Analysis

In addition to helping in the design of accessible central online information resources, the DCP offers usability analysis to departments that are setting up their own online information services. Departmental World Wide Web servers now number over 100 on campus. Usability analysis ensures that users with print impairments will be able to use these resources on an equal basis with their nondisabled peers.

Access to Public and Instructional Computing Facilities

The Office of Academic Computing maintains three public computing facilities for access to Internet resources and numerically intensive computing. Each computing facility has several workstations equipped with motorized, adjustable-height tables for wheelchair accessibility. All lab machines have multimedia cards that allow applications like voice recognition and voice synthesis to be run from any machine in the lab, while all lab machines have 17-inch displays, which help many people with low vision. (Note that these lab computers were not configured with disability access specifically in mind; rather, today's multimedia computers are much more readily and more inexpensively adapted for disability access than their less powerful predecessors.) Where possible, applications like large-print software are run from network file servers. Where additional accommodations are needed, equipment can be installed on an as-needed basis.

Additional public computing facilities are available in the newly renovated undergraduate library. Here a number of workstations are designed for "universal access," with height-adjustable and extra-wide tables, not only for disability access but also for students to work collaboratively. These workstations are configured comparably to those described above, and additional adaptive peripherals are added as needed. All study carrels in the library have laptop Ethernet connectivity. Some of these carrels are adjustable, as are some desks in the public computing area of the reference section.

UCLA has numerous departmental, school, and divisional labs that are not public-access labs. These are used for general and instructional computing. The DCP works with computing support staff in these labs to provide accessibility on an as-needed basis. New lab construction provides the greatest opportunity for building in accessibility at the outset. The newly renovated undergraduate library will have three instructional labs, all designed with accessible aisles and tables.

The DCP encourages these non-public-access or "local" computing centers to support their own users with disabilities, but annual funding cycles can be a barrier to providing prompt access demanded by the academic calendar. The DCP has developed a flexible, rapid-response funding strategy to assist local administrative units in providing computer accommodations in a timely manner. This strategy includes seed equipment, matching funds, and loan equipment which can be purchased by the local unit later, with the funds reverting to the DCP for other purchases, or with the loaner equipment itself returning to a loaner pool managed by the DCP.

Adaptive Computing Technology Research and Demonstration Lab

The DCP's Adaptive Computing Technology Research and Demonstration Lab serves as the focal point for product evaluations, demonstrations, and workshops. Prototype workstations are developed here for departments to emulate. Vendor partnerships result in new and improved products. People with disabilities receive one-on-one consulting and training in the lab. Specialized equipment not yet available in mainstreamed lab settings is also available for drop-in use. For more information, contact:

UCLA Disabilities and Computing Program
Office of Academic Computing
5628 MSA
P.O. Box 951557
Los Angeles, CA 90095-1557
Voice: 310-206-7133
TTY: 310-206-5155
Fax: 310-206-1700
Web: http://www.dcp.ucla.edu

UNIVERSITY OF MISSOURI–COLUMBIA (MU)

In order to meet the adaptive computing needs of people with disabilities in a higher education environment, MU has established the Adaptive Computing Technology (ACT) Center.

The process began in the summer of 1986 when the university formed an ad hoc committee to address the computing needs of the disabled campus population. This committee consisted of representatives from the Access Office for Students with Disabilities, the Academic Skills Learning Center, Special Education, the Office of Equal Opportunity, and Computing Services. Several of the committee's representative departments have contributed financially to the ACT Center's development. Campus Computing provides the majority of the support through integrating adaptive equipment and services into computing campuswide.

In addition, the Center is involved in outreach projects with other members of the original committee. These pilot programs are designed to implement adaptive computing in a variety of nontraditional areas.

The ACT Center's goal is to implement adaptive computing technology in a manner that enhances integration of people with disabilities into the higher education environment. Pursuit of this goal is guided by a holistic model involving a five-pronged approach:

- Increase access to the academic environment. Providing computing access in both general and discipline-specific facilities allows persons with disabilities to utilize the same resources as their nondisabled peers. In addition, incorporating adaptive technology into academic testing empowers students by enabling them to complete examinations independently.
- Provide training. Users gain both a working knowledge of adaptive devices as well as basic computing skills. Those trained fall into three primary groups: people with disabilities; students in disciplines that work with disabled people, such as education, social work, and engi-

neering, who may benefit from adaptive technology applications; and service providers, including computing personnel, rehabilitation professionals, and vocational evaluators.

- Assist faculty in curriculum modification. Ensuring accessibility of academic courseware and basic computing courses aids the integration of persons with disabilities into mainstream campus activities. ACT Center personnel also work with faculty to establish adaptive computing technology as a permanent part of the actual academic curriculum.
- Establish a research emphasis. Identify, evaluate, and develop adaptive computing systems which overcome environmental barriers that exist in higher education and employment settings.
- Facilitate outreach activities. Through disseminating information, awareness is increased on campus, state, and national levels. Advocacy in the areas of acquiring computing funds and access rights is also emphasized.

For more information, contact:

Adaptive Computing Technology Center
200 Heinkel Bldg.
University of Missouri-Columbia
Columbia, MO 65211
Phone: 573-882-2000
Web: http://www.missouri.edu/~ccact/

University of New Orleans (UNO)

The University of New Orleans is committed to making its campus physically accessible and learning accessible for students with disabilities. Two entities have been key in equipping and arranging for assistive technology on campus: the UNO Training and Resource Center for the Blind, established in 1986, and UNO Disabled Student Services, which was first funded in 1988.

The Training and Resource Center for the Blind

The Training and Resource Center for the Blind has been a leading force in bringing assistive technology and instruction to campus and to the surrounding community. It operates under a grant from Louisiana Rehabilitation Services (LRS) and assists clients from UNO and from the greater New Orleans area to develop computer skills and learning strategies to become more independent at home, in school, or on the job. Although the center's primary focus has been vision impairment, it is now serving individuals with hearing and mobility impairments, as well as those with learning disabilities.

The center's classroom computer courses include basic typing, introduction to microcomputing, reservation clerk/customer service, medical transcription, and advanced classes in word processing. Students primarily have vision impairments, although training is also available for persons with other disabilities. Classes are offered throughout the year, based on demand, to LRS consumers. Students can earn high school or college credit. Individualized training can be designed for students with particular needs.

The center has a variety of assistive technology on display in its resource lab. The center is open to consumers, rehabilitation professionals, and educators interested in getting a firsthand demonstration of adaptive devices before purchasing. Staff members are available to assess appropriate assistive technology and provide technical assistance to LRS consumers and UNO students.

The types of assistive technology at the Training and Resource Center for the Blind's resource lab include the following general categories:

- Magnification systems: devices that can magnify printed text or screen images on a computer or closed circuit television.
- Synthetic speech: systems that allows a computer user to "hear" what is on the screen.
- Braille technology: includes Braille displays, translation software, and embossers.
- Optical recognition systems: an optical scanner, special software, and a voice synthesizer that "reads" books aloud.
- Keyboard alternatives: devices such as word prediction programs and voice recognition systems that provide an alternative way to access the computer.

Assistive technology displayed at the Training and Resource Center for the Blind includes low-tech, daily living aids, as well as more advanced computer technology. The resource lab is continually updated as new equipment is developed. In addition to the equipment housed at the resource lab, the center has helped purchase assistive technology for UNO student use elsewhere on the UNO campus, including the Learning Resource Center, the Computer Research Center, and the Earl K. Long Library.

Disabled Student Services (DSS)

The DSS program at UNO serves as a liaison between students and faculty to ensure that appropriate accommodations are provided on campus and in the classroom. This office is the unit designated to meet accessibility requirements under Section 504 of the 1973 Rehabilitation Act.

In 1994, DSS opened the Accommodative Testing and Adaptive Technology Center in the library. Study and testing accommodations are provided there with the assistance of the DSS staff. The Accommodative Testing and Adaptive Technology Center has a number of individual carrels and computers with assistive technology.

On campus, UNO has available magnification systems, synthetic speech, optical character recognition systems, and Braille technology. The Student Government Association recently purchased assistive technology to equip its typing labs.

As on many campuses, the number of students with disabilities has grown considerably at UNO in the past few years. Meeting the accommodation needs of students with vision impairments, learning disabilities, hearing impairments, mobility impairments, and other disabilities is an ever-changing challenge. Extensive use of assistive technology and effective methods of delivering related services has made this challenge a far easier one to meet. For more information, contact:

Training and Resource Center for the Blind
University of New Orleans
P.O. Box 1051
New Orleans, LA 70148
Phone: 504-280-6948; 504-280-5096

Southern Connecticut State University

The Adaptive Technology Lab at Southern Connecticut State University has been in operation since 1989, serving students with learning, vision, physical, and emotional disabilities. The lab consists of 15 workstations and supports Macintosh and IBM-compatible computers, DOS, and Windows. Some of the tables and chairs at the workstations are adjustable. There are a variety of mouse alternatives, alternative keyboards and input devices, and many software choices. The lab is staffed by two part-time staff members, one of whom is released from some teaching duties to direct the lab. They are assisted by a combination of student workers, graduate assistants, and volunteers.

Students are referred to the lab by the Disability Resource Office or by faculty, counselors, or other staff. Some students refer themselves. A student's first task is to complete a two-page intake form, which collects information about the individual's perception of his or her particular problem using computers and prior computing experience. To facilitate future appointments, the student's class schedule is requested. The student is scheduled for an evaluation, which is done on an individual basis with a staff member. Two major decisions are made at that time: What computer platform will the student use, and what adaptive hardware or software is necessary?

Students return for one-on-one instruction, first on the adaptive equipment necessary, and then to learn the necessary computer skills and specific software. Students come for two sessions a week, one to receive instruction and one for "open lab," to practice what was learned. Students receive no credit for their work in the lab. They attend on a voluntary basis to learn skills that will help them be successful in completing requirements for their classes.

When a student and staff member agree that no further instruction is necessary, the student is free to visit the lab anytime "open lab" is scheduled to use the equipment. "Open lab" hours are offered every day but Friday, with some evening hours available. Staff is always present to assist students, not only with computing, but also with writing.

Some of the students with learning or emotional problems need to be taught one-on-one and would not have succeeded (or have already failed) in large computer classes. Some of these students need no special adaptations, and once they know the basics, most are able to use the other computer labs on campus. Some of the other facilities are starting to incorporate adaptive equipment so that students with disabilities have some choices about where to do their work.

The lab has pioneered the teaching of students with learning disabilities in a computer lab. Students with learning disabilities who are placed together in a remedial English composition class are taught word-processing skills along with writing.

The Adaptive Technology Lab serves other functions as well. Education classes at the university frequently visit the lab to learn about the benefits of adaptive technology in teaching students with disabilities. Many of these students return to do projects using adaptive equipment. There is an open house once a month to introduce members of the community to adaptive technology. In addition, the lab staff offers teacher training workshops and in-service programs to teachers from schools around the state. Computer access evaluations are also performed for students referred from public schools and for clients of rehabilitation agencies. Income from evaluations and training support the ongoing operation of the lab. For more information, contact:

Southern Connecticut State University
Adaptive Technology Lab, Buley 22
501 Crescent St.
New Haven, CT 06515
Phone: 203-397-4791

University of Washington (UW)

Adaptive Technology Lab

The Adaptive Technology Lab at UW has received national attention for its resources and services for students, faculty, and staff with disabilities. The lab is included within a large computing facility for all students and is centrally located in the main library on campus. A wide variety of adaptive technologies—both hardware and software—are available for use on a regular basis. Many of the student helpers in the lab have disabilities themselves.

The Adaptive Technology Lab staff help individuals identify systems that will best meet their needs and use them to increase independence, productivity, and success in academic and career pursuits. They also regularly conduct tours of the facility and workshops and demonstrations of the technology that is available to individuals with disabilities.

An innovative and well-received service of the facility is to convert documents into Braille by making use of the campus network. An individual can send an electronic mail message to the Brailling address at the Adaptive Technology Lab. A student helper (usually someone who is blind) converts it into Braille using Braille translation software and an embosser, proofreads and edits it when necessary, and returns the Braille copy to the requester through campus mail, usually within one day of the request. This service is an example of how the University uses technology to streamline services to individuals with disabilities, helps faculty and staff communicate with these people, and makes use of staff with disabilities in delivering these services.

The Adaptive Technology Lab is funded through the same budget as the larger general-access facility and is managed by the central campus computing organization, Computing & Communications (C&C), consistent with the philosophy that computing services for individuals with disabilities should be supported in the same way as computing for those without disabilities. Likewise, at the UW Computer Fair, which features a wide range of computing products and is also managed by C&C, events and exhibits are accessible to individuals with disabilities, alternative formats of publications are provided, and a booth demonstrating adaptive technology increases the awareness of the general public about how people with disabilities can use and benefit from computer and networking resources.

Staff of the Adaptive Technology Lab work closely with the staff of departmental computing labs, the libraries, Disabled Student Services, and other campus units that use computers in order to help them make their facilities, computers, and electronic resources accessible to students, faculty, and staff with disabilities. For example, they promote the development of accessible World Wide Web sites, maintain a model home page demonstrating accessibility features, and provide access to resources that give other units guidance in this area.

For more information, contact:

Information Systems
Computing & Communications
DO-IT
University of Washington
Box 354842
Seattle, WA 98195
Phone: 206-543-0622
Fax: 206-685-4054
Web: http://weber.u.washington.edu/~doit

MODEL LIBRARIES

Bobst Library at New York University, the University of Wisconsin's Stout Library, and the Seattle Public Library have made a particular effort to serve their disabled populations. Two of these libraries are on university campuses and one is a public library.

Bobst Library, New York University (NYU)

With 2.5 million volumes, Bobst is the largest of NYU's eight libraries. The goal of New York University is to provide equal access to this vast store of information for all students and staff. To this end, Bobst Library offers a number of services that can facilitate research activities for those with disabilities.

Center for Students with Disabilities

The staff of the Henry and Lucy Moses Center for Students with Disabilities provides a wide range of services. Each student's needs are assessed prior to enrolling at the university. The resulting written accommodation plan may include such library services as access to adaptive equipment, help in retrieving materials from the stacks, and assistance with photocopying library materials. Most services are available only to students registered with the Center for Students with Disabilities (CSD). CSD services are also available to students temporarily disabled by injuries. Visiting researchers may have materials paged by the library assistant; in the assistant's absence, other staff members are usually available to assist with the retrieval of materials from the stacks.

Librarian for Readers with Disabilities

Bobst has a staff librarian for readers with disabilities who also serves as the library's liaison to CSD. This librarian is available for training sessions in the use of the library's adaptive equipment and for locating materials in alternative formats, including Braille, audiotape, and large print. Bobst also has a library assistant for people with disabilities. The library assistant will:

- Aid students in the use of printed materials.
- Retrieve materials from the stacks, to be picked up at the first floor reference desk.
- Photocopy reserve or microformat materials.
- Assist in obtaining materials through interlibrary loan.

Physical Access to Bobst

Bobst Library was designed as a physically accessible facility. The main floor has level entry through double doors. All levels of the building, except the mezzanine, are accessible by public elevators. Bobst Library also offers wheelchair-accessible telephones, restrooms, and a terminal for Bobst's online catalog.

Reserving Rooms to Work with Readers

Individuals may request access to private study rooms, where they can work with readers, note takers, and other personal assistants. Room reservations can be made in advance, and many rooms are also available on a walk-in basis.

Special Facilities and Equipment

Bobst's Electronic Resources Center houses the library's adaptive computer equipment. The following equipment is available to students registered for services with the Center for Students with Disabilities and to others upon request:

- Kurzweil Personal Reader, which reads text aloud and scans printed materials to disk for a variety of output options (including regular or large print, Braille, or synthetic speech).
- CCTV enlargement system, which uses closed-circuit television technology to magnify print.
- Synthetic speech output for word processing, spreadsheet, and other software applications. In addition, a network connection allows researchers to conduct searches of BobCat (Bobst's online catalog) and other online systems by listening to the content of the computer screen. The system includes VocalEyes and IBM Screen Reader software, as well as a speech synthesizer.
- Large-print computer software, intended for computer users with limited vision.
- A voice input system, enabling users to enter commands verbally, rather than with the traditional computer keyboard. Software, allowing users to convert text files into Grade II (contracted) Braille.

Additional audio equipment, including a Lexicon Vari-Speed Tape Recorder, is located in the Avery Fisher Center at the library.

Services for Hearing Impaired Students

- A portable TDD (Telecommunications Device for the Deaf) is also available; it can be used on any of the library's telephones.
- Closed-caption monitors for viewing video materials are available in the Avery Fisher Center.

For more information, contact:

Disabled Reader Services
Bobst Library
70 Washington Square South
New York, NY 10002
Phone: 212-998-2519

University of Wisconsin-Stout (UW-Stout)

In the 1980s, to enhance library services provided for students with disabilities, the UW-Stout Library designated a new librarian position, assistant to the director for special services. This person was to work cooperatively with other librarians, campus student support staff (including the campus office of services for students with disabilities), and other resources available at UW-Stout, including the Stout Vocational Rehabilitation Institute, the Center for Rehabilitation Technology, and the university's ADA/504 committee.

If a student needs assistance to reach a book from the stacks or is having difficulty deciphering a call number, circulation staff at Stout are available during all hours that the library is open. Individualized consultation services are offered for instruction in the use of adaptive technology equipment or for assistance with any of the library's electronic resources. The assistant to the director for special services works closely with staff of the university's Academic Skills Center, who offer tutoring and writing assistance for students with disabilities. If an assignment involves research, the Academic Skills Center staff and librarian work cooperatively to ensure that the student has access to the library resources needed.

Providing essential services for students with disabilities also depends upon access to the library's resources. The Library Learning Center facility was built in 1982 with a number of features designed to facilitate access for those with physical disabilities. The main entrance has two automatic doors, help phones have been installed at a level within easy reach from a wheelchair, and the stacks have been placed a minimum of 36 inches apart. TTY devices have been installed for incoming calls to the circulation desk and on a pay phone in the lobby for patron use.

In addition, two portions of the circulation desk were modified to provide areas for checking out materials at a height of 28 inches, accessible to someone using a wheelchair. Doorknobs on areas used by the public were replaced with levers that can easily be opened with the "closed fist" method prescribed by the ADA. Display shelving was modified by discontinuing use of the top shelf and thus lowering the highest level of the display to 50 inches, under the ADA maximum requirement of 54 inches.

Easily adjustable tables have been provided for those using wheelchairs in a variety of locations throughout the facility, including the bibliographic instruction room, in reference and periodicals areas, and in the adaptive technology area, where two personal computers provide access to the library's electronic resources.

A wide variety of adaptive technology is used in the Library Learning Center to enhance access to library services and resources for users with disabilities. The most popular and most essential pieces of equipment in this system are the scanning-reading stations. These reading systems are made up of scanners, optical character recognition (OCR) equipment, and software. The readers work in conjunction with a speech synthesizer and screen-reading software.

The reading stations also provide enlargement software and audio access to the library's electronic resources. PubCAT, the online public catalog which includes periodical indexes, is available. In addition, an Internet connection is provided. The Internet connection is especially essential because it provides access to the library's subscription to OCLC's First Search system and to other resources accessible via gopher and the World Wide Web. For more information, contact:

Special Services Librarian
University of Wisconsin-Stout
Library Learning Center 18
Menomonie, WI 54751
Phone: 715-232-1160

Seattle Public Library

The Library Equal Access Program (LEAP)

LEAP was established at the Seattle Public Library in 1987 with funding provided by the Library Services and Construction Act (LSCA) grant. The creators of this program recognized that the library needed to extend beyond its traditional boundaries in order to encourage disabled people to utilize the library services.

The mission of LEAP is to ensure that people with disabilities have open and equitable access to library resources and technology, with or without the assistance of a staff member. While LEAP extends its service to people with a wide range of disabilities, its focus is on those with vision and auditory disabilities.

This program has remained steadfast in adhering to its goals by providing a myriad of services to its patrons, including training on adaptive equipment, assistance on locating and removing material from library shelves and files, and escorting people within the library. LEAP records approximately 140 to 200 visits each month from patrons with disabilities who want to access LEAP equipment. LEAP also provides tours to groups ranging in size from 10 to 60 individuals every few months. The populace served by LEAP resides in the city of Seattle and elsewhere in King County, but there has been a trend in people crossing county lines to access LEAP services.

LEAP has successfully provided adaptive equipment that matches the needs of its patrons. It houses audio and magnification devices that have enabled patrons to access computer software programs. This program has been a catalyst for computer literacy among people with vision impairments. If this program did not have adaptive equipment, many patrons would not be able to access computers because of the high cost of adaptive equipment. The program also features a computerized library catalog with screen magnification and screen reader with synthesized speech, which affords people with vision disabilities access to library resources and the Internet.

The Kurzweil Personal Reader has also been a success with LEAP patrons. This machine scans pages from books, allowing people with vision disabilities access to the printed word. The technology is impressive, but the sheer joy that it brings to patrons is heard in the laughter that comes through the LEAP room door.

The secret to LEAP's success is its belief in human potential and the respect it demonstrates to people who need it. Vision and a sense of humor will allow LEAP to succeed beyond its initial goals. For more information, contact:

Seattle Public Library
Braille Library
821 Lenora St.
Seattle, WA 98121
Phone: 206-386-4690

APPENDIX B

Resources

The Rochester Institute of Technology (RIT) produced a satellite presentation focusing on adaptive technology that removes obstacles to social, employment, and educational access for people with disabilities. The presentation was cosponsored by RIT, the Public Broadcast System, EASI, and the American Association for Higher Education. The resources listed below come from hand-outs that were made available to institutions that supported the satellite broadcast.

ADAPTIVE EQUIPMENT INFORMATION RESOURCES

Closing the Gap Resource Directory

This directory is a comprehensive listing of commercially available hardware and software products identified as appropriate for special education and rehabilitation. It is also included at no extra charge as a part of the *Closing the Gap Newsletter* (see below). Cost is $12.95 plus shipping and handling, obtainable from:

Closing the Gap
P.O. Box 68
Henderson, MN 56044
Phone: 507-248-3294
Fax: 507-248-3810

Closing the Gap Newsletter

Closing the Gap Newsletter reviews software products appropriate for handi-capped and disabled persons and explains in everyday language how this technology is being successfully implemented in education, rehabilitation, and vocational settings around the world. Each issue also contains selected confer-ence proceedings. The *Closing the Gap Resource Directory* (see above) is the February/March issue of this newsletter. A subscription to the newsletter costs $29 in the United States, $44 in Canada and Mexico, and $60 overseas. For more information, contact:

Closing the Gap
P.O. Box 68
Henderson, MN 56044
Phone: 507-248-3294
Fax: 507-248-3810

Co-Net CD-ROM (8th Edition)

This CD-ROM features the complete Cooperative Electronic Library on Disability at a cost of $27 for a single issue or $50 for a two-issue subscription. The library contains:

- ABLEDATA, a database of description and ordering information for over 20,000 assistive technology products, including over 2,500 illus-trations of devices.
- Cooperative Service Directories, which lists thousands of disability-related services by name, type of service, geographical location, and other criteria.
- Publications, Media, & Materials, a database of books, pamphlets, videos, and other information resources on disability, including the 44,000-entry REHABDATA database.
- Text Document Library, which contains complete texts of key dis-ability-related documents providing information on legislation, regu-lations, guidelines, and funding.

For more information, contact:

The Trace Center
University of Wisconsin-Madison
1500 Highland Ave., Room S-151
Madison, WI 53705
Phone: 608-262-6966
Fax: 608-262-8848
TTY: 608-263-5408
E-mail: info@trace.wisc.edu
Gopher/ftp: trace.wisc.edu

ORGANIZATIONS

EASI: Equal Access to Software and Information

An Affiliate of the American Association for Higher Education (AAHE), EASI's mission is to serve as a resource to the higher education community by providing information and guidance in the area of access-to-information technologies by individuals with disabilities. The organization stays informed about developments and advancements within the adaptive computer technology field and disseminates that information to colleges, universities, K–12 schools and libraries and into the workplace.

EASI's members are people from colleges, universities, businesses, and other institutions. They include computing staff, disabled student services staff, faculty, administrators, vendors, representatives of professional associations, private consultants, heads of nonprofit and for-profit organizations, faculty and staff from K–12 schools, and students.

People with disabilities must have the same access to information and resources as everyone else. EASI is dedicated to helping that happen. The organization's activities, projects, and publications listed below are designed to help institutions provide the information and resources that people with disabilities deserve.

National Science Foundation Project

The National Science Foundation funded a two-year grant to the American Association for Higher Education to create materials that will help disabled students study math, science, and engineering. The work was carried out by EASI, and the materials that were developed are based on EASI's ongoing work on adaptive computing technology and access to electronic information for people with disabilities. EASI emphasized using the Internet to distribute this project's work to the largest possible audience.

AAHE and EASI began distributing materials for this project as they were developed. In addition to traditional dissemination methods such as presentations, videos, and publications, EASI distributes materials electronically. Electronic distribution includes an interactive online workshop and the creation of an accessible information database that will make all materials available on gopher.

Internet Discussion Lists

EASI supports three public electronic discussion lists: EASI, AXSLIB-L, and EASI-SEM. These include more than 2,000 people from more than 40 countries. The EASI list focuses on general discussions about adaptive equipment, access issues, and other disability and computer topics. AXSLIB-L is involved with library access issues. EASI-SEM specializes in the dissemination of information and materials to advance access to the fields of science, engineering, and math for students and professionals in those areas.

To join the EASI list, send an e-mail message to: listserv@maelstrom.stjohns.edu. Leave the subject line blank. In the message field, type: **sub easi "firstname lastname"** (put your name in quotes). If you have questions about the EASI list, send them to nmcb@nmsu.edu. To join AXSLIB-L, follow the same procedure as for the EASI list, except in message field, type: **sub axslib-l "firstname lastname"**. Send questions concerning AXSLIB-L to rbanks@discover.discover-net.net. For the list on science, engineering, and math, EASI-SEM, send a message to listserv@listserver.isc.rit.edu. Leave the subject line blank. In the message field, type: **sub easi-sem "firstname lastname"**.

EASI Gopher

EASI information and publications are available through the gopher site at St. John's University. To access EASI information from the gopher, connect to the St. John's gopher, sjuvm.stjohns.edu. From the top menu, choose "Disability and Rehabilitation Resources," and from that menu, choose "EASI."

Electronic Journal

EASI publishes a quarterly electronic journal, *Information Technology and Disabilities*, which focuses on technology issues that relate to people with disabilities. The journal is available through an Internet mailing list. A subscriber can elect to receive either the table of contents and abstracts of articles, or the entire journal. Along with the shorter version, subscribers receive complete information on how to retrieve the full text of articles. To subscribe to the entire journal (75 to 150 pages), send an e-mail message to listserv@maelstrom.stjohns.edu. Leave the subject line blank. In the message field, type: **sub itd-jn "firstname lastname"**. To receive the shorter version, type: **sub itd-toc "firstname lastname"**. These mailing lists are not used as discussion lists. Archived back numbers of *Information Technology and Disabilities* are available through the St. John's University gopher, sjuvm.stjohns.edu. From the top menu, choose "Disability and Rehabilitation Resources," then choose "EASI."

Publications

EASI has created and distributed more than 20,000 publications on adaptive computing technology. Publications are available by contacting easi@educom.edu or through EASI's Web site, http://www.rit.edu/~easi.

Electronic Publications (available through gopher)

Computers and Students with Disabilities: New Challenges for Higher Education (2nd edition)   This provides an overview of how people with disabilities can use computers in postsecondary education. It discusses ideas that campus computing personnel and disabled student service providers can use about campus planning, accessibility guidelines, and legal issues. The publication includes models of five campuses that have made campus computing accessible to people with disabilities.

Computer Access Facts   This four-page brochure is a convenient document for those being introduced to the field of technology for people with disabilities. It gives basic information on disability legislation, demographics, and adaptive computer technology.

EASI Adaptive Computing Self-Evaluation Kit for Colleges and Universities   A 22-page checklist that helps schools evaluate the services they offer disabled students, faculty, and staff. It includes a legal overview, a detailed questionnaire for all departments on a campus, a user-needs checklist, and a short checklist that can be used for the ADA-required self-evaluation of colleges and universities. Offered on a shareware basis. Licensing fee is required.

EASI News for You   EASI's quarterly newsletter, which is sent electronically to list members and on paper to individuals who don't have e-mail.

Opportunities: Equal Access to Electronic Library Services for Patrons with Disabilities   A collection of reprinted articles that discusses providing electronic access for library users.

Equal Access: Information Technology for Students with Disabilities   EASI also has this book available, through the Primis Division of McGraw-Hill. It can be purchased as a complete book or in components. For more information, contact:

McGraw-Hill, Inc.
Primis Division
Princeton Road, S1
Highstown, NJ 08520
Phone: 609-426-5867; 800-962-9342
Fax: 609-426-5900

Seminars   Seminars are offered by EASI that last from one hour to a full day. EASI has made presentations to more than 1,500 people who provide computer and information access to people with disabilities. EASI delivers three-week, online workshops that focus on adaptive computing technology and support services. For information, send e-mail to: listserv@listserver.isc.rit.edu with a blank subject line. Your message should say: **info adapt-it**.

For more information about EASI, contact:

EASI
P.O. Box 18928
Rochester, NY 14618
Phone: 716-244-9065
Fax: 716-475-7120
E-mail: easi@educom.edu
Web: http://www.rit.edu/~easi

The Center on Disabilities at California State University, Northridge (CSUN)

The Center on Disabilities at CSUN was officially formed on May 7, 1993. It is chartered to carry out three major activities:

- Provide services to approximately 800 students with disabilities who are registered with the Office of Disabled Student Services. In addition to such services as counseling, tutoring, and test proctoring, the office also provides computer access assessment and training in its Computer Access Lab.
- Conduct conferences in this country and abroad. The Center currently conducts two major annual international conferences: Technology and Persons with Disabilities, which is held in Los Angeles each March, and Virtual Reality and Persons with Disabilities, which is held in San Francisco each summer.

More than 2,000 persons attend the Los Angeles conference each year, with representation from almost every state and 25 or more foreign countries. About 300 speakers present information. A large exhibit area houses about 140 stations, and there are numerous new product announcements made each year as a part of this conference.

The Virtual Reality conference deals with the specialized area of virtual reality and its potential with people with disabilities. Science fiction writer Ray Bradbury has been one of its keynote speakers. About 300 people attend. A growing number of new technological applications in the field of disability are showcased at this conference each year.

The Center also conducts special meetings from time to time on issues of particular interest. In 1991, for example, the center conducted a workshop in Palm Springs, California, on voice input/output, which resulted in the identification of eight national priorities. The proceedings of this conference, featuring a keynote address by Tony Vitale of Digital Equipment Corporation, was published and distributed widely.

The Center publishes proceedings of all of its conferences, which are made available in print and electronic formats.

- Engage in a variety of research and training projects. Past projects include training in assistive technology and in learning disabilities throughout federal Region IX: California, Arizona, Nevada, Hawaii, Guam, Saipan, and American Samoa; development of a screen-reading device for learning disabled persons; and development of a universal access system and research into three technologies of benefit to learning disabled users.

The center also conducts a one-week training program, Leadership and Technology Management (LTM), designed to stimulate systems change; that is, activities that will lead to the acquisition and use of more technology by more persons with disabilities. The LTM training program is funded in part by California's State Tech Act grant. A limited number of scholarships are available to California residents under this grant. Those from outside California may be considered on a tuition basis.

For more information on CSUN's Center on Disabilities, contact:

Center on Disabilities
California State University, Northridge
18111 Nordhoff St.
Northridge, CA 91330-8340
Phone, V/TDD, Message: 818-885-2578
Fax: 818-885-4929
E-mail: LTM@csun.edu

HEATH Resource Center

The HEATH Resource Center is a clearinghouse that operates under a federal legislative mandate to collect and disseminate information nationally about disability issues in postsecondary education. Funding from the U.S. Department of Education enables the center to increase the flow of information about educational support services, policies, and procedures related to educating or training people with disabilities after they have left high school. The HEATH Resource Center's goals are:

- To identify and describe educational and training opportunities.
- To promote accommodations that enable full participation by people with disabilities in regular, as well as specialized, postsecondary programs.

- To recommend strategies that encourage participation in the least restrictive and most productive environment possible for each individual.

To accomplish these goals, HEATH has an extensive publication program, a toll-free telephone service, and a professional staff that participates in a strong network of colleagues across the country.

HEATH produces a newsletter that is published three times a year and is distributed nationally, free of charge, to subscribers. The newsletter highlights campus programs, provides information about new or pending legislation, and offers reviews of new publications and other media products. HEATH resource papers, monographs, guides, and directories focus on disability-related issues as they emerge on college campuses or in vocational-technical training schools, adult education programs, independent living centers, and other community-based training programs. Single copies of HEATH publications are free and may be reproduced. Most are available by request on audiocassette tape or computer disk.

HEATH's main constituency includes postsecondary school administrators and service providers, teachers and instructors, high school and vocational rehabilitation counselors, government officials, librarians, health professionals, and journalists, as well as those with disabilities and their families. A toll-free telephone line is available to encourage direct interaction with HEATH staff.

Participation by HEATH staff in national, regional, and statewide conferences and training workshops has led to the development of a national network of professionals across the nation. This network enables staff to suggest speakers, access options, audiovisual materials, and other resources to enhance such meetings. For more information, contact:

HEATH Resource Center
One Dupont Circle, Ste. 800
Washington, DC 20036
Phone/TTY: 800-544-3284
Phone (Washington, DC): 202-939-9320

RESNA

RESNA serves as an information center to address research, development, dissemination, integration, and utilization of knowledge in rehabilitation and assistive technology. For more information, contact:

RESNA
1700 N. Moore St., Ste. 1540
Arlington, VA 22209-1903
Phone: 703-524-6686
TTY: 703-524-6639
Fax: 703-524-6630

Trace Research and Development Center

The Trace Center is an interdisciplinary research, development, and resource center on technology and disability, based in the Waisman Center and the Department of Industrial Engineering at the University of Wisconsin-Madison. The mission of the center is "to advance the ability of people with disabilities to achieve their life objectives through the use of communication, computer and information technologies."

The Trace Center was founded in the early 1970s, focusing on the communication needs of people with severe physical disabilities. It was an early leader and innovator in the field that came to be known as "augmentative communications," a term that came out of the Trace Center's writings. Among its early achievements was the development of the first portable, user-programmable electronic communication device for nonspeaking people.

At the time of the emergence of the personal computer, the Trace Center became involved in making computers accessible to people with disabilities. Starting with a 1984 White House meeting on the topic, the center served as coordinator for the nationwide Industry-Government Initiative on Computer Accessibility. The guidelines developed through this initiative have been widely used in the computer industry, both as design criteria and as a means for measuring how well individual products accommodate users with disabilities.

The Trace Center has worked directly with computer companies to integrate disability access features into their standard, mass-marketed products. As a result of this work, disability access features are now being incorporated directly into most of the major operating system environments in the computer industry, including Macintosh OS, DOS, Microsoft Windows, and Windows NT, IBM OS/2, and UNIX/X-Windows.

Recently, the Trace Center has begun to focus on the accessibility problems of newer generation information and transaction systems. As these systems become more widespread in education, employment, and daily life, their accessibility to people with disabilities becomes critical. In 1993, the Trace Center was designated as the national Rehabilitation Engineering Research Center on "adaptive computers and information systems" by the National Institute on Disability and Rehabilitation Research, U.S. Department of

Education. Using the collaborative model it established with the computer industry, the Trace Center aims to work with consumers and the information industries to ensure that people with disabilities have equal access to new information technologies and the emerging information "superhighway."

Selected Trace Center Projects Relating to Electronic Access, Standards, and Guideline Development

Accessible Human Interface Design   The Trace Center has developed a number of disability extensions to the human interface of standard computer operating systems. These extensions have often been developed first as models and demonstrations, then actually implemented in standard product design for the operating systems. Over the past eight years, seven basic features have been designed, including keyboard access to mouse functions, adjustment of keyboard response characteristics for those with movement or coordination difficulties, visual indications of warning beeps for users with hearing impairments, and auditory indication of visual indicators for users who are blind.

Macintosh OS Access Program   The Trace Center has worked with Apple Computer in its accessibility efforts. A suite of features called Easy Access, based on Trace Center feature designs, was first released as part of the Macintosh operating system in 1987. Since then, Easy Access has been part of every Macintosh computer sold.

DOS Access Program   Working with IBM Corporation, the Trace Center created a set of basic accessibility features for IBM computers using DOS. The software, known as AccessDOS, is currently available from IBM free of charge as an add-on to DOS. Plans call for integrating it directly into DOS, so it is available on all systems.

Microsoft Windows Access Program   The Trace Center has developed the Windows Access Pack, providing a set of access features similar to AccessDOS for the Microsoft Windows operating environment. Microsoft Corporation is now incorporating these directly into Windows Version 4.0 and the newer Windows NT.

Disability Access Committee for X (DACX)   The Trace Center serves as the coordinator for this industry-consumer-researcher committee, which is seeking to make the industry standard X-Windows interface accessible. This opens up operating systems such as UNIX to people with disabilities. The DACX includes the Trace Center, MIT, Georgia Tech, Digital Equipment Corporation, Sun Microsystems, IBM, Berkeley Systems, AT&T, and others.

Seamless Human Interface Protocol   This protocol being developed by the Trace Center will make most current and developing information technologies more accessible to people with disabilities. It defines standard ways of interacting with information technologies—such as automated teller machines, information kiosks, and interactive television systems—so that people with disabilities can use the same tactics to access different systems in different environments.

Design Guidelines Series   Over the past 10 years, the Trace Center has developed a number of design guidelines for accessibility of products. These guidelines focus on how the user controls the product and how the product provides information feedback to the user. They deal with a full range of disability needs, including hearing impairment, blindness, and physical impairments. The guidelines have been widely used within industry and have also been used as the basis for developing access regulations.

Computer Design Guidelines   This first set of guidelines grew out of the efforts of the Industry-Government Initiative on Computer Accessibility, coordinated by the Trace Center. They have been widely used by computer companies as a guide to making sure their products are accessible to users with disabilities.

Software Design Guidelines   Under a commission from the Information Technology Association (formerly ADAPSO), the Trace Center is working with consumers and developers to create a set of guidelines for making standard software applications more accessible to people with disabilities. Over 1,000 copies of an initial version were distributed by ITA. The Microsoft Corporation distributed another 5,000 copies to its Windows developers.

Consumer Product Design Guidelines   With assistance from the Assistive Devices Division of the Electronic Industries Association, the Trace Center has developed and disseminated a set of accessibility guidelines for consumer electronic products.

Communication Product Guidelines   The Trace Center is working to develop a series of specific, focused guidelines dealing with telephones, fax machines, voice mail, VCRs, televisions, and photocopy machines.

Standards Development

The Trace Center has developed several electrical and electronic standards related to products for people with disabilities.

Electrical Interface Transducer Standard   This standard defines electrical connections for switches and other interfaces to assistive technologies. It is now used by the majority of makers of these devices.

General Input Device Emulating Interface (GIDEI) Standard   The GIDEI Standard defines the interface between special input devices for people with disabilities and standard mass-market computers. It is now used with all PCs made by major companies and is compatible with any programmable devices with serial output.

Serial Wheelchair Control Interface Standard   At the request of several assistive technology manufacturers/clinicians, the Trace Center initiated the development of a standard for controlling wheelchairs through external electronic devices such as communication aids. Together with the RESNA wheelchair committee, the Trace Center developed a draft standard, which has now been picked up by the International Standards Organization.

Information Libraries and Database

Cooperative Electronic Library on Disability   The Trace Center is working on a cooperative effort to create an electronic library of information resources on disability. The library is available through a variety of channels, including CD-ROM and the Internet. Access for users with disabilities is being integrated into the software.

Database of Disability-Related Products   The Trace Center has developed an extremely user-friendly yet accessible interface for a major public database of over 19,000 assistive technology products (ABLEDATA). This software is now distributed to over 1,000 sites nationwide and is fully accessible in both its character-based and graphic forms to people who are blind.

Cooperative Service Directories   This Trace Center software lets organizations develop and distribute electronic directories of disability-related services. The CSD software resulted from a cooperative effort with over 30 disability information centers nationwide.

Interstate Taxonomy of Disability Services   In cooperation with national and state organizations, the Trace Center is structuring a system for categorizing disability services. The standardization has allowed the exchange of data between states.

Publications, Media, and Materials Database

This new software allows information on disability-related books, articles, videos, and other media to be easily stored and retrieved. It is being used as one of the tests of the Trace Center's Seamless Human Interface Protocol.

Trace Resource Book

Over the past two decades, the Trace Center has regularly published printed comprehensive directories of products related to communication, control, and computer access for people with disabilities. Now in its 6th edition, the Trace Center's *ResourceBook* is a standard reference for available products in these fields. For more information about the Trace Center, contact:

University of Wisconsin-Madison
1500 Highland Ave., Room S-151
Madison, WI 53705
Phone: 608-262-6966
Fax: 608-262-8848
WWW, Gopher, and ftp servers: trace.wisc.edu

World Institute on Disability

The World Institute on Disability (WID) is a public policy, research, and training center dedicated to independence for all people with disabilities. WID's goals are to:

- Empower people with disabilities to take control of their own lives.
- Challenge attitudes that stereotype people with disabilities as unable to participate fully in society.
- Change public policies that keep people with disabilities dependent at home or in institutions.
- Teach people with disabilities to define and communicate their own desires and needs.
- Educate the public, policymakers, businesses, and the media about people with disabilities and independent living.
- Train today's and tomorrow's leaders of the disability rights movement.

Facing the Facts

What do people with disabilities want? What do people with disabilities need? The answers WID has uncovered are familiar—work, play, families, friends, and choices. But people with disabilities often need support to reach these goals. That support ranges from assistance with getting out of bed to laws guaranteeing physical access to buildings and public transportation.

Action research takes WID directly to people with disabilities to answer these and many other questions. And because more than half of WID's staff and board are disabled, they know what to ask. WID finds out how people with disabilities want to live. They identify the supports that will enable people with disabilities to achieve their life goals and dreams. Then they take this information to policymakers; corporate, community, and disability leaders; the media; and the public.

By working with these individuals and groups, WID challenges the stereotypes of people with disabilities—stereotypes that often lead to unemployment, lack of opportunities, and discrimination.

One of WID's goals is to provide accurate information for public and private policy makers to use in crafting services and policies that support independence and quality of life. In the public sector this can mean services that promote employment, accessible buildings, and community involvement. In the private sector this can mean policies that accommodate people with disabilities in the workplace and as customers. WID's research findings and educational materials are also used by an extensive network of disability organizations to promote an agenda of independence and change.

Meeting the Challenge

WID's projects support its mission of independence for all people with disabilities through working with a variety of individuals and groups.

Education and Training   WID's leaders travel throughout the country and around the world to educate policymakers, corporations, foundations, and the media about the empowerment of people with disabilities.

Personal Assistance Services (PAS)   Personal assistants help disabled people with their daily activities—from dressing and household chores to balancing a checkbook. Through research and education, WID is working with a grassroots coalition of nonprofits and policymakers to design more effective publicly-funded PAS programs. The coalition's goal is to redirect public dollars to create a system that supplies personal assistants to more of the people who need them. **International Training and Education**   WID hosts foreign visitors and sends staff and outside representatives to other countries to work with disability organizations worldwide on issues, training, and information exchange. Through IDEAS (International Disability Exchange and Studies), WID and Rehabilitation International awards grants to individuals who visit other countries to study disability-related policies and programs. The information is published and made available to policymakers to use in addressing similar issues and programs in the U.S. These international activities are funded by the federal government. **Research and Training Center on Public Policy in Independent Living** Funded by the U.S. Department of Education, the Center conducts research and training on major policy issues including: personal assistance services, independent living, leadership development, and community integration, with the goal of creating dynamic new approaches that maximize self-sufficiency for people with disabilities.

For more information about WID, contact:

World Institute on Disability
510 16th St.
Oakland, CA 94612-1500
Phone: 510-763-4100
TTY: 510-208-9493
Fax: 510-763-4109

APPENDIX C

Manufacturer Addresses
A Concise Guide to Alternative Input/ Output Software for IBM-Compatible PCs

This information has been compiled by Kaitlin Computer Consultants and is a condensed version of the Kaitlin Guide. For more information on purchasing the complete Kaitlin Guide, contact:

Kaitlin Computer Consultants
18 Stephanie Ave.
Nepean, Ontario K2E 7A9
Canada
Phone: 613-224-73980
E-mail: kaitlin@magi.com

This list is not comprehensive; rather, it is an overview of some of the possibilities. Exclusion from this list should not be interpreted as an indication that a product is unsuited for its advertised task, nor does inclusion constitute endorsement of a product. If possible, test competitive products before buying (demonstration versions are sometimes available).

Kaitlin Computer Consultants assumes no responsibility for product claims made by manufacturers and cannot guarantee that the information represents the most recent version of the software. You are advised to call the manufacturer or dealer for complete technical specifications, prices and availability. Product names used in this guide are trademarks of their respective manufacturers. This guide does not deal with hardware devices.

Abacus (NoMouse)
5370 52nd St. SE
Grand Rapids, MI 49512
Phone: 800-451-4319

Access Technology (J.A.M., SofType)
8445 Keystone Crossing, Ste. 165
Indianapolis, IN 46240
Phone: 317-465-1275

ACON (ApS Software, KeepKey)
P.O. Box 843
2400 Copenhagen NV
Denmark

AI Squared (Zoom Text, VisAbility)
P.O. Box 669
Manchester Center, VT 05255-0669
Phone: 802-362-3612

Arkenstone (An Open Book Unbound)
1390 Borregas Ave.
Sunnyvale, CA 94089
Phone: 408-245-5900; 800-444-4443

Artic Technologies (Business Vision, Magnum GT, Win Vision)
55 Park St.
Troy, MI 48083
˙Phone: 810-588-7370

ARTS Computer Products (PC Braille, PC Sift, WP Sift)
P.O. Box 604
Cambridge, MA 02140
Phone: 770-482-8248; 800-343-0095

Berkeley Systems (OutSpoken for Windows)
2095 Rose St.
Berkeley, CA 94709
Phone: 510-540-5535

Burnett, Jeffrey (Dwell Pick)
School of Architecture
Washington State University
Pullman, WA 99164-2220
Phone: 509-335-1937

Creative Labs (VoiceAssist)
1901 McCarthy Blvd.
Milpitas, CA 95035
Phone: 408-428-6600; 800-998-5227

Davids, Noah (RunHere)
6115 East Surrey Ave.
Scottsdale, AZ 85254

Dragon Systems (DragonDictate)
320 Nevada St.
Newton, MA 02160
Phone: 617-965-5200; 800-825-5897

EuroCom (ECMenu)
P.O. Box 293
CH-6900 Massagno
Switzerland

Grabowski, Dave (FIXINI)
9 Sussex Ave.
Newark, NJ 07103-3926

GW Micro (VocalEyes)
310 Racquet Dr.
Fort Wayne, IN 46825
Phone: 219-489-3671

Henter-Joyce (JAWS)
2100 62nd Ave. North
St. Petersburg, FL 33702
Phone: 813-572-8900; 800-336-5658

HumanWare (MasterTouch)
6245 King Rd., Ste. P
Loomis, CA 95650
Phone: 916-652-7253; 800-722-3393

IBM Corporation (AccessDOS, VoiceType Dictation)
Special Needs Information and Referral
4111 Northside Parkway
Atlanta, GA 30321
Phone: 800-426-2133

Innovative Designs (Finish Line)
2464 El Camino Real, Ste. 245
Santa Clara, CA 95051
Phone: 408-985-9255

JRE Enterprises (Win Multiple)
Configurations
P.O. Box 5643
Mesa, AZ 85211-5643

Konz, Ned (Lens)
1400 Gandy Blvd., No.1213
St. Petersburg, FL 33702-2131

Kurzweil Applied Intelligence (Kurzweil Personal Reader)
411 Waverley Oaks Rd.
Waltham, MA 02154
Phone: 617-893-5151

Leotti, George (Dragger)
416 S. Elmwood Ave.
Glenolden, PA 19036-2327

Microsoft Corporation (AccessPack for Windows)
One Microsoft Way
Redmond, WA 98052-6399
Phone: 206-637-7098

Microsystems Software (HandiCHAT, HandiCODE, HandiKEY,
   HandiSHIFT, HandiWORD, MAGic)
600 Worcester Rd.
Framingham, MA 01701
Phone: 508-626-8511; 800-828-2600

MicroTalk (ASAP)
917 Clear Creek Dr.
Texarkana, TX 75503
Phone: 903-832-3471

OMS Development (EEK, TinyTalk)
610-B Forest Ave.
Wilmette, IL 60091
Phone: 847-251-5787; 800-831-0272

Optelec (LP-DOS)
P.O. Box 729
Westford, MA 01886
Phone: 800-828-1056

Prentke Romich (KeyREP)
1022 Heyl Rd.
Wooster, OH 44691
Phone: 800-642-8255; 800-262-1984

Raised Dot Computing (MegaDots)
408 South Baldwin
Madison, WI 53703
Phone: 608-257-9595; 800-347-9594

Schipperheijn, J. (Gaze)
Postbus 1494
5602 BL Eindhoven
The Netherlands

Simmons, John (SoftSwitch)
51 Bendigo Ave.
Bentleigh, Victoria 3204
Australia

Syntha-Voice Computers (Slimware Window Bridge)
800 Queenston Rd., Ste. 304
Stoney Creek, Ontario L8G 1A7
Canada
Phone: 905-662-0565

Tash (JDN Shorthand)
Unit 1, 91 Station St.
Ajax, Ontario L1S 3H2
Canada
Phone: 905-686-4129; 800-463-5685

TeleSensory (OsCaR, Vert)
455 N. Bernardo Ave.
P.O. Box 7455
Mountain View, CA 94039-7455
Phone: 415-960-0920; 800-227-8418

Verbex Voice Systems (Listen for Windows)
1090 King George Post Rd., Bldg. 107
Edison, NJ 08837
Phone: 908-225-5225; 800-ASK-VRBX

Virtual Magic Software (Magic Desk)
P.O. Box 12264
Huntsville, AL 35815-0264

Words+ (Equalizer, EZ Keys for Windows)
43700 17th St. West, Ste. 202
P.O. Box 1229
Lancaster, CA 93584
Phone: 805-266-8500; 800-869-8521

XEROX Imaging Systems (Reading AdvantEdge)
9 Centennial Dr.
Peabody, MA 01960
Phone: 508-977-2000; 800-248-6550

BIBLIOGRAPHY

Apple Computer Worldwide Disabilities Solutions Group. *Independence Day: Designing Computer Solutions for Individuals with Disabilities.* Cupertino, CA: Apple Computers, 1990.

Architectural and Transportation Compliance Board. *Uniform Federal Accessibility Standards.* Washington, DC: Architectural and Transportation Compliance Board, 1993.

Barry, William A.; John A. Gardner; and Randy Lundquist. "Books for Blind Scientists: The Technological Requirements of Accessibility." *Information Technology and Disabilities* 1, no. 4, 1994. Special issue: Access to Math, Science and Technology by Persons with Disabilities.

Berliss, Jane. *Checklists for Implementing Accessibility in Computer Laboratories at Colleges and Universities.* Madison, WI: Trace Research and Development Center, University of Wisconsin-Madison, March 1991.

Brown, Carl. *Computer Access in Higher Education for Students with Disabilities.* 2nd ed. Sacramento: High-Tech Center for the Disabled of the California Community Colleges Chancellor's Office, 1989.

Computer and High Technology Grants. Research Grant Guides. Tallahassee, FL: State of Florida: 1991.

Directory of Building and Equipment Grants. Research Grant Guides. Tallahassee, FL: State of Florida: 1991.

EASI. *Computer Access Facts.* Los Angeles: Project EASI, 1992.

EASI. *Computers and Students with Disabilities: New Challenges for Higher Education.* 2nd ed. Los Angeles: Project EASI, 1992.

Flechsig, Scott; and Richard Jones. *Converting Text to Braille.* Los Angeles: EASI, 1993.

Handicapped Funding Directory. Research Grant Guides. Tallahassee, FL: State of Florida: 1991.

HEATH. *Information from HEATH.* (A monthly newsletter.)Washington, DC: HEATH Resource Center.

Heinisch, Barbara Schiller. "Establishing an Adaptive Technology Laboratory in a University Setting." *Technology and Disability* 1992, 47–54.

Hilton-Chalfen, Danny; and Carmela Castorina. "Looking Ahead: Federal Legislation and Campus Computer Access for People with Disabilities." *EDUCOM Review* Fall/Winter 1991.

IBM National Support Center for Persons with Disabilities Resource Guides for Persons with Disabilities (Hearing Impairments, Learning Impairments, Mobility Impairments, Speech or Language Impairments, and Vision Impairments). Atlanta, GA: IBM, 1991.

Information Technology and Disabilities. This electronic journal (ISSN 1073-5127) is published quarterly by EASI. See Appendix B for details on how to subscribe and how to obtain archived articles.

Jones, Richard. *Converting Graphical Information to Raised Line Drawings.* Los Angeles: EASI, 1993.

King, Warren; and Jane Jarrow. *Testing Accommodations for Students with Disabilities.* Columbus, OH: AHEAD, 1992. Available from AHEAD, P.O. Box 21192, Columbus, OH 43221; phone 614-488-4972; fax 614-488-1174.

Lunney, David. "Assistive Technology in the Science Laboratory: A Talking Laboratory Work Station for Visually Impaired Science Students." *Information Technology and Disabilities* 1, no. 4, 1994. Special issue: Access to Math, Science and Technology by Persons with Disabilities.

Murphy, Harry. *The Impact of Exemplary Technology-Support Programs for Students with Disabilities.* Northridge, CA: National Council on Disability, 1992.

National Science Foundation. *Changing America.* Washington, DC: National Science Foundation, 1989.

Raman, T. V. "AsTeR: Audio System for Technical Readings." *Information Technology and Disabilities* 1, no. 4, 1994. Special issue: Access to Math, Science and Technology by Persons with Disabilities.

Scott, Neil G. *Computer Assistance for People with Disabilities.* San Francisco: DeskTop Marketing, Inc., 1987.

Shell, Duane F.; Christy A. Horn; and Mary K. Severs. "Effects of a Computer-Based Educational Center on Disabled Students' Academic Performance." *Journal of College Student Development* 29, September 1998, 432–40.

Skawinski, Warren J.; Thomas J. Busanic; Ana Ofsievich; Victor Luzhkov; and Carol Venanzi. "The Use of Laser Stereolithography to Produce Three-Dimensional Tactile Molecular Models for Blind and Visually Impaired Scientists and Students." *Information Technology and Disabilities* 1, no. 4, 1994. Special issue: Access to Math, Science and Technology by Persons with Disabilities.

Southern Connecticut State University. *Adaptive Technology Lab Start-up Kit.* New Haven: Southern Connecticut State University, 1992.

Williams, John; and Chet Nagle. "The ADA—An Analysis: What Will the Americans with Disabilities Act Mean to You?" *Careers and the Disabled* 6 (63), 4.

INDEX

by James Minkin